Cindy
Thanks for your
Love +
Support

I MUST LOVE ME

A journey to self-acceptance and unconditional self-love

I MUST LOVE ME

A journey to self-acceptance and unconditional self-love

UNIQUE PARSHA

Copyright © 2024 UNIQUE PARSHA

All rights reserved.

No part of this book may be reproduced, stored in a retrieval system, or transmitted, in any form or by any means, electronic, mechanical, photocopying, recording, or otherwise, without prior written permission from the publisher, except for brief quotations embodied in critical reviews and certain other noncommercial uses permitted by copyright law.

ISBN: 978-1-963949-65-0 (Paperback)
ISBN: 978-1-963949-66-7 (Hardcover)

Printed in the United States of America

DEDICATION

IN LOVING MEMORY OF......

Brenda Washington, Jackie O, and Roni Spivey, your radiant presence left an indelible mark on my heart. Your unwavering love and boundless affection illuminated every corner of my world. I'm grateful for the kindness and support you offered, serving as steadfast allies in the journey of life. Your absence leaves a void beyond measure, yet your love remains alive within me. Rest peacefully, knowing you're forever loved.

My two fathers, Earnest Taylor and Dennis Parsha, your absence is deeply felt, reminding me of the profound impact you had on my life. Memories of your culinary delights and infectious smiles remain vivid in my mind and bring warmth to my heart. You may be gone from this world but the love you extended to me continues to be a guiding light in the journey of life.

Myrtle Lee Hildreth and Wilie Lee Parsha, my cherished grandmothers, your love formed the very foundation of my being. From the moment I entered this world, your unwavering affection and guidance have shaped my path, and I carry the cherished memories of shared nights and extended phone conversations close to my heart. Though you are physically gone, your presence lies on in the love you bestowed upon me.

Betty Gaines, your affection and support were a constant source of strength and comfort tome. You were an exceptional godmother to my son and a true mother figure who treated me like your own daughter. Your unconditional love, presence, and readiness to help whenever needed have left a special mark on my heart, for which I will be forever grateful.

My niece Janae Rice, you will forever be in my heart. Rest Well! Everyone misses you so much.

This book is the result of a collective effort, reflecting the love, support, and encouragement of all those mentioned above. To all those not explicitly named, your contributions, big or small, have played a role in shaping this journey and have not gone unnoticed. You have made a significant impact on the success of this project and I am profoundly grateful for your presence in my life. I am humbled to share this work with the world.

With heartfelt appreciation,

Unique Parsha

ACKNOWLEDGMENT

I am deeply grateful to God, whose divine guidance and presence have illuminated every step of my journey and bestowed upon me immeasurable blessings.

To my precious children, Ja'waun, Ja'Ken, and G'nelle, you are the light of my life and the greatest blessings I have ever known. Your love, laughter, and boundless energy bring joy to my days, and I am endlessly grateful for the privilege of being your parent. G'nelle I'm beyond proud of you at UCLA attending one of the best and hardest colleges to get into. You have been a straight A student throughout all your school years. You're the best daughter that I could ask for or ever want. Continue to achieve goals and follower your dreams like your mother.

To Vishal, your boundless love and guidance were invaluable, and you still hold a special place in my heart. You were my steadfast supporter, my rock in times of need, and your presence brought light into my life. You were the first person to hear of my goals and dreams and have always been there to support me every step of the way. I will forever love you and cherish our memories.

To my wonderful sisters, Yvonne Rice, Marceth James, Gwendolyn Horton, Keela Page, and Jamilla Calhoun, your love, support, and unwavering belief in me have been a constant source of strength and inspiration. Your presence in my life enriches my days and fills my heart with gratitude. I know I drive you all crazy being spoiled, a brat, and demanding.

To my beloved brother, Mathew Rice and sister n law Yvonne, Your affection, love, support, and encouragement have been a wellspring of inspiration, guiding me through life's challenges with love, wisdom, and harsh words. Our closeness, reminds me of the depth of love and connection we share, bringing joy into my life. Thanks for everything you did for me, always showing up when I need you, and always willing to help me at any given time and I'm very thankful.

To my cherished extended family-The Parsha's, Hildreth's, Taylor's, and my beloved family in Mississippi, The Washington Family, and The Rice Family-your love, encouragement, and solidarity have been pillars of strength throughout my journey.

Special thanks to Debra Wade for embracing the role of a godmother to my sons wholeheartedly and always being there when we needed you. I will love you forever and cherish everything. RIP (Ron Wade) my son God-father and the entire Wade family.

Mark and Damina (My brother and sister), your presence in my life has been a blessing beyond measure. As siblings, you have become like family to me, offering support, love, and companionship. Your encouragement and solidarity have touched my heart deeply and enriched my life in countless ways. Here's to the bond we share and the many more memories we'll create together. We turn up whenever we get together.

Valentino & Valerie Smith, you have been important pillars of strength to me, and I deeply appreciate your presence in my life. During times of need, you have stood by my side, offering support, kindness, and love without hesitation. I genuinely cherish the bond we share and am grateful for the enduring friendship we have cultivated. I'm forever grateful!

Darlena Mays, your incredible love and support have been a constant source of comfort, strength, and inspiration in my life. I am profoundly grateful for the significant role you've played in shaping my journey. Your friendship means the world to me and I am blessed to have you in my life. Showing up at the hospital unexpectedly and helping me at my lowest point. You have been amazing to me, and I'm forever thankful.

My best friend, My brother, and My son's God-father, Pastor Greg Hunter, your presence in my life has been a blessing beyond measure. Your faith, wisdom, and support have been instrumental in shaping my journey. You have stood by me through thick and thin, offering guidance and encouragement when I needed it most. Your friendship is a cherished gift, and I am grateful for your continued presence in my life. We might fight like cats and dogs, disagree, and cuss each other out but, at the end of the day, it's nothing but love between us. It used to be You, Roni, and I clued to each other and on the phone with each other ALL day. In honor of Roni, he would want us to stay close and I know this is what he wanted because he talked about it to me numerous of times. He wanted me to forgive you of the things that I'm hurt about and did say that you were wrong. I love you with all of my heart and even when I'm mad at you, I still love you.

To my church family at Acts Full Gospel and The Reconditioned Church, your unwavering faith, fellowship, and support have been a constant source of solace and inspiration. Your prayers, encouragement, and love uplift my spirit and strengthen my resolve, fostering a sense of community and belonging that I cherish deeply.

This book is the result of a collective effort, and I am indebted to each and every one of you for making it a reality. Thank you for being a part of this incredible journey.

With profound appreciation,

Unique Parsha

INTRODUCTION

Greetings to all the remarkable souls out there! Get ready to embark on a transformative journey towards embracing your true self and nurturing unbreakable self-love. In the pages of this captivating book, "I Must Love Me, "Unique Parsha, the creative genius behind "The Pink Lady of Oakland" and "Love N Me," unveils the key to unlocking the incredible power of self-acceptance and genuine self-love.

Are you ready to break free from the chains of societal expectations, media pressures, and the longing for external validation? As you delve into this enchanting work, you'll discover a path that leads to unshakable self-worth, a profound connection with your uniqueness, and an unwavering love for the person you are becoming. The journey towards becoming your own biggest supporter starts now, and it's going to be an exhilarating ride.

In a world that often magnifies insecurities and encourages conform it, Unique Parsha's wisdom shines as a beacon of authenticity and self-assurance. In these pages, you'll find the tools to rise above the noise and celebrate your individuality with confidence. It's time to embrace every facet of yourself-the quirks, the curves, the dreams, and the doubts-because that's what makes you truly exceptional.

Throughout the following chapters, we will delve into the vital topics that matter most as you navigate the path of self-discovery and empowerment, from the overwhelming influences of social media to the essential importance of valuing your body and your mind.

We'll discuss the transformative power of embracing your unique qualities and understanding your worth. You'll learn how to navigate the pitfalls of comparison, stand strong in the face of external pressures, and unapologetically be yourself. Along the way, we'll explore the magic of feminine energy, the significance of healthy relationships, and the profound impact of self-acceptance. And, of course, we'll delve into the heart of self-love, discussing techniques to boost your self-esteem, foster confidence, and build unbreakable self-trust.

As you embark on this journey through "I Must Love Me, "you'll be equipped with the knowledge, insights, and tools to navigate the challenges that arise as r in today's world. By the time you finish reading, you'll not only recognize your own unique brilliance but also understand that your journey to self-adoration is ongoing, exciting, and deeply rewarding.

So, my dear adventurers, are you ready to embark on a journey of self-discovery, empowerment, and love? Open the pages of "I Must Love me" and let the transformation begin. The voyage toward embracing your true self and nurturing self-love starts now-get ready for a journey that will illuminate your path for years to come.

TABLE OF CONTENT

Dedication i
Acknowledgment iii
Introduction vii
Chapter 1: Self Love 1
   What Is Self-Love? 2
   The Abc's Of Self-Love:
   A Journey To Empowerment And Fulfillment 6
   The Power Of Self-Love In Empowering Women.............. 17
   The Essence Of Love:
   Empowering Women To Embrace Self-Love 20
   Experimenting With Self-Love 23
   The Self-Love Experiment Process 28
   The Essence Of Self-Love 29
Chapter 2: Self Acceptance 34
   The Magic Of Self Acceptance 39
   A Story Of Strength And Resilience: Learning To Walk Alone 45
   Embracing The Journey To Being Comfortable In Your
   Own Skin 51
   Embracing Your Worth: A Guide To Self-Value And
   Empowerment For Women 54
   The Magic Of Self-Trust 66
Chapter 3: Beauty And Fashion 74
   Discovering Your Value: A Guide To Realizing Your
   Self-Worth 80
   How To Value Yourself: The Art Of Sele-Valuation 89
Chapter 4: Self Development 92

Be You: Be Unapologetically You! 99

Self-Development Secrets: How To Cultivate A Better You!! 107

A Guide To Self-Esteem And Increasing Your Confidence!! 115

Embracing Self-Compassion And Self-Care.................................... 123

Chapter 5: Transforming Pain Into Power: 126

Introduction: 127

Chapter 6: Feminity 131

What Is Feminity... 132

The Magic Of Feminine Energy!!.. 140

Chapter 7: Women In Social Media... 149

The Real Story Behind The Images 155

Chapter 8: Embrace Your Battle: Choose Your Struggle 162

Why Is Sex Important?... 165

Communication About Needs And Desires 176

Navigating Menopause With Self-Love:
A Comprehensive Guide For Women... 179

Chapter 9: Sexual Wellness And Well Being 185

Empowering Wellness:
Understanding Mental Health In Women!!..................................... 186

Mental Health Conditions Specific To Women 186

Know Your Worth:
A Guide To Healthy Relationship Standards!! 194

A Guide To Identifying And Exiting Abusive Relationships!!........ 201

Chapter 10: Mental Health 209

The Struggle For Wholeness:
Empowering Women To Break Cycles And Cultivate Self-Love ... 218

Chapter 11: A Woman's Guide To Fearless Independence
And Ambition 225

Chapter 12: Dealing With Pain 240
    Embracing Your Body 241
    Forged In Fire: The Phoenix Rising 245
Conclusion 250
About The Author 258

SELF LOVE?

What is Self-Love?

Nowadays, one undoubtedly recognizes the importance of self-care as a necessary technique not only for individual development but also as a measure of mental well-being. At the same time, the term appears to be both simple and complex to the extent that one can have many different opinions about it. In question, it is no longer a single word but rather symbolizes the complicated ensemble of feelings, ways of thinking, and manners of discourse where I am the one who is addressed. However, after the supporters of the strategy present their side, the opponents counter their arguments, saying that the implementation process is rather far-fetched and that the consequences may not be as satisfying. The proponents of the approach, on the other hand, purport it is a key requirement for individual rights' fulfillment and happiness. Hence, to fully realize the essence of true self-love, very careful research is needed (Deniz & Yildirim Kurt ulus, 2023). This investigation encompasses the elements of a definition, psychological aspects, and empty manifestations.

The purest form of self-love occurs at the personal level, that is, the interplay of holding oneself in high regard, having self-compassion, and accepting oneself. Such a self-care practice involves a sort of relationship with the person in which one demonstrates patience and kindness to oneself. It calls for the fact that you have to remember you are valuable because it is different in you that you have something special you are talented in. What may look merely as an outermost recognition of something, this recognition is more complex as it goes deep into the soul, and one may also become conscious of the inner strengths and weaknesses of a person. The rationale presented is not narcissistic or arrogant but is rather a product of acknowledging one's human nature and the worth that every individual possesses simply by being a person.

Yet, the arduous path of self-love is riddled with dips, and the obstacles are generally self-constituted, mainly leaning on the individual's personal perception of themselves rather than external forces. A lot of our narratives in culture regard self-love - a form of narcissism or selfishness, and so if someone loves him or herself, that is seen as a negative trait. The latter is compounded by the third party's mockery and humiliation, manifesting in loss of self-esteem and a sense of shame. Furthermore, there is the perception of perfection and judging oneself against others that start the unending process where one greatly looks for standards that are not attainable, then on to self-criticism and dissatisfaction (Harshad & Ghosh, 2022). As a result, the struggle with self-love becomes a complex task that is not only the reflection of society through the resolution of the contradicting norms but also the scrutiny of self-misconceptions.

Through a psycho-sociological approach, self-love is connected with some key notions, for example, self-esteem and self-efficacy, which demonstrate the complexity of the topic. In self-love, the sources of this feeling lie entirely within oneself, being generally self-generated, irrespective of other people.

Today, I believe self-esteem is more connected and dependent on what other guys think of you and what achievements you have made. The treatment of self-kindness demonstrates love and compassion, which is a catalyst for the learning of new skills through any kind of adversity that might occur. Furthermore, individual confidence, which is the base of the capacity to face criticism and challenges and change directions according to the goals, is another advantage of self-love. Although the commonly held point of view of the romantic notion of self-love is that it is entirely positive, this does not tell the whole truth; it would be better for us to reconsider this notion to know clearly what the fate of the idea is after it has been materialized. People are afraid that those who think of themselves as a final aim may feel entitled and lazy. Those people may be unwilling to work and achieve something meaningful. These feelings, in another way, make them justify themselves in not improving in some directions or seeing their disadvantages. Another important factor is the way the product of self-love is marketed by the commercial society, which is of great significance in this process. By turning this idea into a marketable commodity and missing the point of deeper human purpose, the marketing tricks ultimately encourage more superficial ways of living (Duvallet, 2020).

Consequently, the indiscriminate or immature kind of love that self-directed love does not offer may be judged and undervalued. It could be interpreted as a mere fashion statement with the metamorphosis being neglected and overlooked.

Moreover, although the intersectionality of self-love makes its application more difficult because of the many cultural and social contexts, which in turn demand a much deeper analysis, it is a critical factor in self-love promotion. First, people who believe in self-love think that self-care is valuing everyone the same way. Some revolutionaries, on the other hand, believe that it is particular to some cultures and contains implicit biases. The self-esteem and sense of satisfaction of a person with his/her self-worth and social acceptability are socially learned, and, therefore, cultural norms and social institutions determine which forms of self-love are considered appropriate in a given society. Therefore, it is far from adequate to use a generalized way of being self-love since self-love is affected by the complexities of identity and privilege, which means that an analysis of the contextual relevance and ethical implications of self-love is needed.

Nonetheless, in spite of the uncertain circs and the disagreements, it's an undeniable, nonetheless significant one to be of self-love. It brings peace of mind and gives a reason for the rocking boat, the mood of the hustle and bustle of modern existence. It becomes a transformational power that exceeds the limits of the world of that person, which is able to create rational compassion and empathy toward other people. It is by working through their personal emotional hurdles and achieving emotional resilience and sincerity that people become capable of creating interactions and a society that has meaning (Utami et al., 2023). The essence of this concept is that it is a correlative movement not only for personal liberation but also for the betterment of society as a whole and for the creation of a world that is more tolerant and empathetic.

Self-love, in the end, is nothing like a simple commodity of narcissism or selfishness, as one might assume. Rather, it is a multi-dimensional reality that goes beyond the normal beliefs about it. The major message of the poem is that via the practice of fortitude and the energy of resistance to a calamity, one comes to experience the full depth of one's own value as well as individual distinctiveness. In this respect, the implementation of its principles carries along a number of issues and discrepancies, which is indeed a matter of serious thought in so far as the social and psychological aspects of it are concerned. Step by step, over cultural barriers and acceptance of differences, self-love is transformed into a liberating factor that can lead to both individual and community liberation. Therefore, the process of loving oneself will be considered to be an existential aim, perpetually infused with not only complexity but also an element of great significance, and it will help a great deal in the understanding of the human condition.

The ABC's of Self-Love: A Journey to Empowerment and Fulfillment

In a world that often teaches women to prioritize the needs and expectations of others above their own, the concept of self-love emerges as a beacon of empowerment and resilience. "I Must Love Me," a book dedicated to exploring the intricate journey of women towards self-acceptance and inner strength, delves deep into the transformative power of self-love.

"I Must Love Me" beautifully encapsulates this transformative journey, offering invaluable insights and practical guidance for women seeking to embark on their path towards self-love. Through poignant narratives and empowering exercises, the book invites readers to embark on a journey of self-discovery, acceptance, and unconditional love.

Introduction:

In the intricate path of discovering oneself and growing as a person, lies a radiant treasure-a deeply meaningful essence that unlocks our contentment and strength: self-love. Often overlooked or misunderstood, self-love is the cornerstone of a fulfilling and empowered life. In the symphony of existence, they are the notes that compose the melody of our inner harmony, guiding us towards a deeper understanding of our worth, the ABC's of self-love can pave the way to a deeper sense of worth, confidence, and happiness.

Self-love, the cornerstone of personal fulfillment, thrives on the ABC's of A, B, and **Acceptance** is the foundational step towards self-love, encapsulated in the Letter A. It entails embracing all aspects of oneself, flaws and strengths alike, fostering a sense of inner peace and contentment. Moving to the letter B **Believing in**

oneself is paramount for nurturing self-love. When one learns to recognize their inherent beauty and worth, even in moments of doubt, they pave the way for profound self-compassion and empowerment. Finally, C represents **Confidence**, the fuel that propels self-love forward. Being confident not only allows individuals to assert their boundaries and pursue their aspirations fearlessly but also fosters a deep sense of self-assurance and respect. Together, these ABC's form a powerful toolkit for cultivating self-love, enabling individuals to navigate life with grace, resilience, and an unwavering appreciation for their unique selves.

For women particularly, the importance of self-love cannot be overstated. In a society often plagued by unrealistic standards of beauty, success, and womanhood, women face relentless pressure to conform, leaving little room for self-compassion and authenticity. However, it is precisely amidst these societal expectations that self-love becomes an indispensable tool for reclaiming one's worth and forging an unapologetically authentic path.

Self-love empowers women to break free from the shackles of perfectionism and comparison, embracing their unique journey with grace and resilience. It instills the courage to set boundaries, prioritize self-care, and pursue passions unapologetically. Through self-love, women learn to silence the inner critic and celebrate their strengths, fostering a profound sense of inner peace and fulfillment.

Let's embark on this transformative odyssey-a sacred quest to explore the depths of self-love, letter by letter, and unravel the mysteries that lie therein. Every single letter in the alphabet contains a divine message, a guiding light that leads us towards self-discovery and the ultimate truth.

Acceptance: The First Step Towards Self-Love

In the vast expanse of the human experience, one of the most profound journeys we undertake is the journey towards self-love. It's a journey that begins with acceptance, the cornerstone upon which genuine self-love is built. Acceptance is not merely about acknowledging the positive aspects of ourselves; it's about embracing every facet of our being, including the parts we may deem imperfect or flawed.

Acceptance is a radical act of self-love. It requires us to embrace ourselves exactly as we are, without judgment or condemnation. It means acknowledging our strengths and weaknesses, our triumphs and failures, and recognizing that each aspect contributes to the richness of our human experience.

Acceptance is not resignation or complacency. It's not about settling for less or giving up on growth and improvement. Instead, acceptance is about acknowledging reality as it is, without resistance or denial. It's about making peace with our past, forgiving ourselves for our mistakes, and releasing the burden of regret and shame.

Embracing Imperfection - In a world that often glorifies perfection, accepting our imperfections can be a radical act of self-love. It's about embracing our flaws and vulnerabilities, recognizing that they are an integral part of what make us human. Our imperfections are not something to be ashamed of; they are what make us unique and authentic.

When we embrace our imperfections, we free ourselves from the unrealistic expectations and standards imposed upon us by society or ourselves. We no longer strive for an unattainable ideal of perfection but instead embrace our humanity in all its messy, beautiful complexity.

Letting Go of Comparison - Comparison is the thief of joy and a barrier to self-acceptance. When we constantly compare ourselves to others, we diminish our own worth and value. Acceptance requires us to let go of the need for comparison and recognize that we are enough just as we are.

Instead of measuring ourselves against others, we can celebrate our own journey and accomplishments. We can recognize that each of us is on a unique path, and there is no one-size-fits-all definition of success or fulfillment. When we let go of comparison, we create space for self-love to flourish.

The Power of Forgiveness - Central to acceptance is the power of forgiveness - both forgiving ourselves and others. Holding onto grudges and resentments only serves to weigh us down and hinder our ability to love ourselves fully. Forgiveness is not about condoning past actions or absolving others of responsibility; it's about releasing ourselves from the grip of anger and bitterness.

When we forgive ourselves, we acknowledge that we are human and prone to mistakes. We recognize that we are worthy of compassion and understanding, despite our flaws. And when we forgive others, we release ourselves from the burden of carrying around resentment and anger.

Consider the story of Emily, who spent years battling with feelings of inadequacy and unworthiness due to past mistakes. However, through the practice of acceptance, she came to realize that her worthiness was not contingent upon her past actions. By embracing acceptance, Emily found the courage to forgive herself and move forward with compassion and grace.

Emily's Journey Unveiled: A Simplified Tale of Resilience and Empowerment

Acceptance is the first step on the journey towards self-love. It's about embracing ourselves fully, flaws and all, and recognizing our inherent worth and value as human beings. When we practice acceptance, we free ourselves from the chains of self-criticism and judgment, and open ourselves up to a life of greater joy, fulfillment, and love. So let us embark on this journey of self-acceptance with open hearts and minds, knowing that it is the key to unlocking the boundless potential within ourselves.

Believe In Yourself: A Woman's Journey to Empowerment, Self-Respect and Well-Being

In the labyrinth of life, there exists a guiding light - an unwavering belief in oneself that illuminates the path to empowerment and fulfillment. For women navigating the complexities of societal expectations and personal aspirations, this belief is not just a luxury but a necessity - a beacon of strength and resilience in the face of adversity. In this chapter, we delve into the transformative power of self-belief, exploring its profound impact on the lives of women and the journey to embracing one's true potential.

Believing in oneself is more than just a fleeting moment of confidence; it is a deep-rooted conviction that resonates within the core of our being. It is the unwavering faith that we are capable, worthy, and deserving of success, happiness, and fulfillment, regardless of the doubts and skepticism that may surround us.

For women, self-belief serves as a revolutionary act - an assertion of our inherent worth and value in a world that often seeks to diminish or dismiss our contributions. It is a declaration of our right to dream, to aspire, and to carve out our own paths, unapologetically and authentically.

In a society rife with gender bias and stereotypes, women often find themselves facing doubt and skepticism from external sources - from colleagues who question their abilities, to family members who underestimate their ambitions. Yet, it is precisely in these moments of doubt that our belief in ourselves becomes most vital - a shield against the arrows of criticism and a source of inner strength.

Consider the story of Maya, a young entrepreneur with a bold vision to disrupt the male-dominated tech industry. Despite facing resistance and skepticism from investors and industry insiders, Maya remained steadfast in her belief in herself and her vision. Through unwavering determination and resilience, she defied the odds and built a successful startup, inspiring a new generation of women to pursue their entrepreneurial dreams.

Believing in oneself is not just about external validation or accolades; it is about cultivating inner resilience and fortitude in the face of adversity. It is about recognizing that setbacks and failures are not reflections of our worth but opportunities for growth and learning.

Believing in oneself is not just a personal journey; it is a ripple effect that extends far beyond our own lives, inspiring and empowering others along the way. When women embrace their inner worth and potential, they become beacons of light, guiding others towards their own paths of empowerment and self-discovery.

Think of the countless trailblazers throughout history who dared to believe in themselves and their visions, from pioneering scientists and inventors to groundbreaking artists and activists. Their unwavering belief in themselves and their abilities has left an indelible mark on the world, inspiring generations of women to embrace their own power and potential.

Embrace Your Power - In conclusion, believing in oneself is not just a luxury but a necessity for women navigating the complexities of life. It is a declaration of our inherent worth and value, a shield against doubt and skepticism, and a source of inner strength and resilience. So let us embrace our power, dear sisters, and believe in ourselves with unwavering conviction, for in doing so, we unlock the door to infinite possibilities and pave the way for a future where all women can thrive and soar to new heights of empowerment and fulfillment.

Confidence: The Heartbeat of Self-Love

Confidence - the radiant glow that emanates from within, illuminating the path to empowerment and self-assurance. For women navigating the complexities of life, confidence is not just a trait but a powerful tool - a source of strength and resilience in the face of adversity. In this chapter, we delve into the transformative power of confidence, exploring its profound impact on the lives of women and the journey to embracing one's true potential.

Confidence is more than just a superficial facade; it is a deep-rooted belief in oneself and one's abilities. It is the unwavering assurance that we are capable, competent, and deserving of success and happiness, regardless of the challenges that may lie ahead. For women, confidence serves as a catalyst for growth and self-actualization - a beacon of light guiding us towards our dreams and aspirations.

In a world that often seeks to diminish or dismiss the contributions of women, self-doubt can be a formidable adversary - a shadow that lurks in the recesses of our minds, casting doubt upon our worth and potential. Yet, it is precisely in these moments of doubt that our confidence becomes most vital - a shield against the arrows of criticism and a source of inner strength.

Confidence is not just about external validation or accolades; it is about cultivating inner strength and resilience in the face of adversity. It is about recognizing that setbacks and failures are not reflections of our worth but opportunities for growth and learning.

Confidence is also about embracing authenticity and owning our unique strengths and qualities. It is about celebrating our individuality and refusing to conform to societal expectations or norms. When we embrace our true selves with confidence and self-assurance, we inspire others to do the same, creating a ripple effect of empowerment and liberation.

Think of the countless trailblazers throughout history who dared to be confident and unapologetically themselves - from pioneering scientists and inventors to groundbreaking artists and activists. Their confidence and authenticity have left an indelible mark on the world, inspiring generations of women to embrace their own power and potential.

In conclusion, confidence is not just a trait but a mindset - a way of being in the world that empowers us to embrace our true selves and pursue our dreams with courage and conviction. So let us step into our power, dear sisters, and embrace confidence as our birthright - a source of strength and resilience that guides us towards a future where all women can thrive and soar to new heights of empowerment and fulfillment.

"Believe you can, and you're halfway there." - Theodore Roosevelt

The Reward of Self-Love: Unveiling the Empowered Self - Self-love, a radiant beacon amidst life's tumultuous seas, bestows upon us a treasure trove of rewards - a sacred gift that reverberates through every facet of our existence. As we embark on the journey of self-discovery, we unlock the boundless potential that lies within, empowered by the transformative magic of self-love.

Self-love is a radiant gift, empowering us in myriad ways:

- Discover Your Authentic Self: Embrace your uniqueness, unveiling the raw beauty within.
- Know Your Narrative: Rewrite your story with courage, reclaiming your truth.
- Nurture Your Nature: Cultivate your innate gifts and passions, allowing them to flourish.
- Question Negativity: Challenge limiting beliefs, embracing your worth and potential.
- Feel Your Feelings: Honor your emotions as messengers of the soul, embracing authenticity.
- Dream Daily: Dare to envision a future without limitations, nurturing your aspirations.
- Listen to Your Intuition: Trust the guiding wisdom of your inner voice, navigating with clarity.
- ·Move Your Mind and Body: Embrace mindful movement, honoring the sacred union of body and spirit.

In the embrace of self-love, we unlock boundless potential, discovering our truest selves and embracing life's journey with open hearts and minds.

In the concept of self-love, we have covered the basic ideas of acceptance, limits, and compassion. - Each serving as a guiding light on our journey of self-discovery and empowerment. We have delved into the depths of acceptance, embracing our imperfections with grace and compassion, and recognizing our inherent worthiness as human beings. We have erected the sturdy walls of boundaries, safeguarded our well-being and preserved our sense of identity and autonomy. And we have nurtured the tender heart of compassion, extending kindness, understanding, and empathy to ourselves and others alike.

Through these practices, we have uncovered the transformative power of self-love - a power that transcends the boundaries of time and space, and resonates deeply within the core of our being. We have learned that self-love is not a destination to be reached, but a journey to be embraced - a journey of growth, healing, and self-discovery.

As we stand at the threshold of our own evolution, let us remember that self-love is not a solitary pursuit, but a collective endeavor - a shared journey of humanity. Let us reach out to one another with open hearts and open minds, offering support, encouragement, and understanding along the way. Let us celebrate our victories and acknowledge our struggles, knowing that each step forward is a triumph of the human spirit.

In the face of adversity and uncertainty, let us anchor ourselves in the principles of acceptance, boundaries, and compassion, drawing strength from the wisdom of our own hearts. Let us remember that self-love is not a luxury, but a necessity - a vital force that sustains us through life's myriad challenges and triumphs.

In essence, self-love is not a destination but a continuous journey of self-discovery and growth. It is a radical act of courage and defiance in a world that often seeks to diminish our worth. "I Must Love Me" stands as a testament to the unwavering resilience and inherent worth of every woman, reminding us that true empowerment begins with embracing the boundless depths of self-love.

And so, dear reader, I invite you to take these principles to heart, to embody them in your daily life, and to share them with others as you continue on your own journey of self-love. For in doing so, you will not only transform yourself but also contribute to the collective healing and evolution of our world.

May you walk this path with courage and grace, knowing that you are worthy of love and deserving of all the blessings life has to offer. And may you always remember that the greatest journey of all is the journey back to yourself - a journey fueled by the boundless power of self-love.

THE POWER OF SELF-LOVE IN EMPOWERING WOMEN

In the journey of life, amidst the chaos and clamor, there exists a profound essence that often gets overlooked - the essence of self-love. It's not just a fleeting notion or a trendy catchphrase; it's a profound force that has the power to transform lives, especially those of women. To women everywhere, I extend an invitation to explore this sacred path, for within its folds lies the key to unlocking your inner radiance and empowering your spirit. Self-love is the radiant light that shines from within, illuminating every aspect of our being with acceptance, compassion, and unwavering belief in ourselves.

WHAT IS SELF-LOVE, YOU MAY ASK?

What is self-love? It's the gentle embrace we offer ourselves when we stumble and fall, the empowering voice that whispers, "You are enough," in a world that constantly tries to convince us otherwise. It's the unshakeable foundation upon which we build our dreams and the guiding compass that leads us toward authenticity and fulfillment.

For women, self-love is not just a luxury; it's a revolutionary act of defiance against the oppressive narratives that seek to diminish our worth and confine us to narrow boxes of acceptability. It's a declaration of sovereignty over our bodies, minds, and spirits, reclaiming the right to define ourselves on our own terms.

But self-love is more than just a solitary pursuit; it's a collective movement that thrives on solidarity and sisterhood. When we lift ourselves up, we create a ripple effect that lifts others along with us, forging bonds of mutual support and empowerment that transcend boundaries and barriers. Self-love is not merely a fleeting indulgence or a superficial embrace of one's physical attributes. It is a profound recognition of your worth, a celebration of your essence, and a commitment to nurturing your soul. It is the gentle whisper that reminds you of your inherent beauty, strength, and resilience. It is the unwavering conviction that you are deserving of love, not only from others but, most importantly, from yourself.

So how do we cultivate self-love in a world that often seems intent on eroding it? It begins with a radical act of self-awareness, a willingness to look within and confront the layers of conditioning and self-doubt that have accumulated over time. It requires us to challenge the toxic messages that tell us we're not good enough, not pretty enough, not worthy of love and respect.

Self-love means setting boundaries that honor our needs and priorities, saying no to anything - or anyone - that diminishes our sense of self-worth or compromises our well-being. It's about nurturing our bodies with nourishing food, movement, and rest, recognizing that we deserve to be treated with kindness and care.

But perhaps most importantly, self-love is a practice of forgiveness - forgiving ourselves for our perceived shortcomings, mistakes, and failures. It's understanding that we are human, imperfect beings, worthy of love and belonging just as we are. Know that you are enough, just as you are, in this moment and every moment thereafter. You are worthy of love, respect, and kindness, both from others and from yourself. Embrace your uniqueness, your quirks, your passions, for they are the colors that paint the canvas of your life with vibrancy and vitality.

PRACTICING SELF-LOVE

Practicing self-love is a daily commitment - a series of small, intentional acts that nourish our minds, bodies, and souls. It starts with setting boundaries that protect our energy and prioritize our well-being. It means saying no to things that drain us and yes to activities that bring us joy and fulfillment. Self-love is about tuning into our intuition and honoring our inner voice, even when it goes against the expectations of others.

Self-love also involves embracing self-care as a sacred ritual rather than a luxury. It's about carving out time for rest, reflection, and rejuvenation, knowing that we cannot pour from an empty cup. Whether it's practicing mindfulness, journaling our thoughts, or engaging in creative expression, self-love invites us to connect with ourselves on a deeper level and cultivate a sense of inner peace and balance.

To all the women reading this, know this: You are magnificent. You are powerful beyond measure. You are worthy of love, respect, and all the blessings life has to offer. Embrace your radiance, dear sisters, and let it shine brightly for all the world to see. For in loving yourself, you inspire others to do the same, and together, we rise.

THE ESSENCE OF LOVE: EMPOWERING WOMEN TO EMBRACE SELF-LOVE

In a world teeming with complexities, love stands as a beacon of light, guiding us through the darkest of times and illuminating our path towards fulfillment and self-discovery. Love, in its purest form, transcends boundaries, defies conventions, and empowers us to become the best versions of ourselves. In this discourse, we delve into the essence of love, exploring its transformative power, and how women can harness it to cultivate self-love and empowerment.

1. UNDERSTANDING THE ESSENCE OF LOVE

Love, often misconstrued as a mere emotion, is a profound force that permeates every facet of our existence. It encompasses compassion, empathy, and understanding, fostering connections that transcend superficialities and endure the test of time. At its core, love emanates from within, radiating outward to envelop our surroundings with warmth and acceptance.

For women, embracing the essence of love begins with recognizing their inherent worth and embracing their individuality. Society often imposes unrealistic standards and expectations, leaving many women feeling inadequate and unworthy of love. However, true love knows no bounds and flourishes in the fertile soil of self-acceptance and authenticity.

2. EMPOWERING WOMEN THROUGH SELF-LOVE

Self-love is the cornerstone of empowerment, serving as a catalyst for personal growth and fulfillment. To love oneself is to acknowledge one's strengths and imperfections alike, embracing them as integral components of the beautiful tapestry that is the self.

Empowered women understand that their worth is not contingent upon external validation but stems from a deep-seated belief in their inherent value.

Cultivating self-love requires introspection, compassion, and a willingness to embark on the journey of self-discovery. It involves nurturing oneself physically, emotionally, and spiritually, prioritizing self-care and setting boundaries that honor one's needs and desires. Through self-love, women reclaim their autonomy and assert their right to lead fulfilling lives on their own terms.

3. NAVIGATING THE LANDSCAPE OF RELATIONSHIPS

In the pursuit of love, women often find themselves navigating a complex landscape fraught with challenges and uncertainties. It is imperative to discern between genuine affection and superficial infatuation, choosing partners who uplift and respect them unconditionally. Love should never be synonymous with sacrifice or compromise; rather, it should elevate and enrich both parties involved.

Moreover, women must recognize that they are deserving of love in its purest form - a love that honors their worth, celebrates their uniqueness, and nurtures their growth. They must refuse to settle for anything less than they deserve, trusting in their intuition and embracing their inherent value.

However, the path to self-love is often paved with obstacles - doubt, insecurity, and the weight of societal expectations. Yet, in the face of adversity, there lies an opportunity for transformation. Empowerment blooms from the seeds of self - awareness, nurtured by compassion and self-care. It is in the gentle embrace of self-love that women discover their inherent worth, reclaiming their narratives with fierce determination.

Yet, the journey of self-love transcends individual empowerment; it is a collective awakening, a ripple effect that permeates through communities and generations. As women, we hold the power to inspire and uplift one another, to cultivate a culture of love and acceptance. In celebrating our unique journeys, we pave the way for others to embark on their own path towards self-discovery.

In essence, love is the most powerful force in the universe, capable of transforming lives and transcending barriers. For women, it serves as a source of strength, resilience, and empowerment, propelling them towards self-discovery and fulfillment. By embracing the essence of love and cultivating self-love, women can embark on a journey of empowerment, unlocking their true potential and inspiring others to do the same. Remember, dear women, you are worthy of love in its purest form - embrace it, cherish it, and let it guide you on the path to self-discovery and empowerment.

EXPERIMENTING WITH SELF-LOVE

This whole cycle of self-love - falling in love with yourself and then figuring out how to keep that love alive - is crucial and it's a process that's satisfying because we suddenly discover a nicer, kinder way of life. One in which we are no longer at odds with ourselves but embrace ourselves with love. Imagine living a life free of pressure to modify or improve yourself. You don't feel compelled to be unique, fit in, or be accepted since you know you're enough. I feel this style of life, which is the subject of this book, is perfectly attainable.

Experimenting with Self-Love: A Journey to Inner Fulfillment

The journey of self-love is a profound cycle - a continuous process of falling in love with oneself and nurturing that love to keep it alive. It's a journey that leads us to a more satisfying way of life, one where we no longer find ourselves in opposition to our own being, but instead, we wholeheartedly embrace ourselves with love.

Imagine a life unburdened by the constant pressure to modify or improve yourself. A life where you don't feel compelled to conform, fit into predefined molds, or constantly seek external acceptance because you wholeheartedly believe in your intrinsic worth.

The essence of this book is centered on the possibility of living this way. It's a life where self-love is not just a concept but a lived reality. It's attainable, and it begins with you.

In the chapters that follow, we'll delve into the intricacies of self-love, exploring its transformative power and providing practical guidance on how to nurture and sustain this beautiful love affair with yourself. This book is an invitation to embark on a journey of self-discovery, self-acceptance, and inner fulfillment. Get ready to explore the path to a life where self-love reigns supreme.

Uncovering the Layers of Self-Love

Self-love, as you'll discover in the following chapters, is a multifaceted gem. It's not a one-size-fits-all concept but rather a deeply personal experience. In this journey, we'll peel back the layers of self-love to reveal its true essence.

Understanding Your Intrinsic Worth

One of the foundational pillars of self-love is recognizing your inherent worth. You'll learn to see yourself through a new lens - one that acknowledges your unique qualities, strengths, and imperfections as valuable components of your identity.

Nurturing Self-Compassion

Self-love thrives on self-compassion. We'll delve into the art of treating yourself with the same kindness and understanding you offer to others. You'll discover that self-compassion is not a sign of weakness but a source of profound strength.

The Power of Authenticity

Embracing authenticity is a pivotal step in your self-love journey. We'll explore how being true to yourself and owning your uniqueness is not just liberating but also deeply empowering.

Breaking Free from External Expectations

External pressures and societal expectations often hinder our ability to love ourselves fully. You'll learn strategies to break free from these constraints and live a life aligned with your true self.

Practicing Self-Care and Setting Boundaries

Self-love is inseparable from self-care. We'll discuss the importance of nurturing your physical, emotional, and mental well-being.

You'll also gain insights into setting healthy boundaries that protect your self-love.

Embracing Body Diversity and Rejecting Unrealistic Standards

Our journey of self-love extends to embracing our bodies as they are, rejecting society's unrealistic beauty standards, and cultivating a positive body image

The Journey to Self-Value

Recognizing your inherent worth and practicing self-respect by setting boundaries are integral to building a strong foundation of self-value.

Cultivating Self-Care Habits: Nurturing Your Well-Being

Self-love finds its home in self-care. In this chapter, we'll explore the importance of self-care practices, setting boundaries, and prioritizing your well-being.

Finding Joy in Your Own Company: Learning to Love Yourself

The final chapter will invite readers to find joy in their own presence and bask in the beauty of self-compassion. It's a celebration of the love affair one has cultivated with oneself.

Throughout this book, readers will uncover the depths of self-love and, in doing so, embark on a journey to inner fulfillment. Get ready to embrace this transformative path one that begins and ends with oneself, a journey where self-love truly reigns supreme.

Embarking on a journey filled with self-discovery, growth, and the pursuit of dreams is a universal experience. But amidst this transformative period, one challenge often stands out: the pressure to conform to societal expectations, especially in the realm of relationships. This chapter is here to remind readers that individuality is the greatest strength. It's time to break free from the mold, assert uniqueness, and thrive in adulthood.

Embracing Your Individuality

In a world that sometimes feels overrun by societal norms and the opinions of others, it's easy to lose sight of what makes you, well, you. But here's the truth: each one of you is a one-of-a-kind masterpiece, a tapestry of thoughts, emotions, and experiences that no one else can replicate. Your individuality is a treasure, and it's time to celebrate it.

Discuss the Uniqueness of Each Individual

Let's begin by acknowledging the incredible diversity that exists among us. Each person is a unique blend of talents, interests, and passions. No two individuals are exactly the same, and that's a beautiful thing. It means that your journey in life is unlike anyone else's, and it's tailor-made for you.

The Self-Love Experiment Process

Self-love began from a place where there was a lack of self-care and love towards oneself The body called out for attention, signaling a need for recognition, affection, and care, despite not fully grasping the concept of body love initially. It was a body that, despite its size, desperately sought to be acknowledged and cherished independently. It was a call for attention that had been ignored, physically uncomfortable, and challenged by everyday spaces like airplane seats.

Embracing all facets of oneself is essential in the journey of self-love. This story isn't just about one's body-though "the body" plays a crucial role as it carries one through life. It's about facing fears to foster learning and growth. For some, the challenge might be their relationship with their body, their relationship status, feelings of being off track, or discomfort with a part of themselves or their appearance. This feeling of isolation in struggle is not unique.

The Self-Love Experiment is beneficial for anyone who has felt the need to "fix" something within themselves or in someone else. Striving for something we lack, like happiness, peace, or love, through alteration, repair, or manipulation only perpetuates a cycle of discontent. It's an endless chase, enticing yet ultimately unsatisfying, leaving one feeling cold and alone after the pursuit. This endless pursuit is a trap, fostering a continuous search for "something more," which becomes a habitual craving.

To break free from this cycle, it was crucial to reevaluate daily practices and prioritize self-care, stepping away from the relentless pursuit of an unattainable "there."

THE SELF-LOVE EXPERIMENT PROCESS

DURATION: THREE MONTHS

GOALS

- Cultivate a lighter being (emotionally, physically, spiritually, and intellectually).
- Enhance self-confidence to ensure that reflections in the mirror are met with kindness.
- View oneself through the adoring eyes of one's dog - awesome, amazing, beautiful, and quite possibly the coolest person in the world.

THE ESSENCE OF SELF-LOVE

In the intricate tapestry of human emotions, love reigns supreme as the most profound and transformative force. It emanates from the depths of our souls, intertwining with every facet of our existence. Yet, amidst the clamor of external expectations and societal pressures, it is often the most fundamental form of love - the love we harbor for ourselves - that is overlooked. For women across the nation, the voyage toward empowerment commences with the profound understanding and embrace of self-love.

The essence of self-love transcends mere sentiment; it is a state of being to be fully embodied. It is a profound recognition of our intrinsic worth, a jubilant celebration of both our strengths and our imperfections. It is a journey that commences with a solitary stride - a stride towards acceptance, compassion, and forgiveness. Through the journey of self-love, we not only pave the way for a brighter, more fulfilling future for ourselves but also for women nationwide, as we collectively embark on the odyssey of embracing the quintessence of our own divine worth.

"If you want to love others, your love for your own self should be on top," whispers the timeless wisdom of the sages. These words echo resolutely through the chambers of our hearts, serving as a poignant reminder that love originates from within. It transcends the boundaries of mere self-indulgence or vanity; it is a profound acknowledgment of our innate value. To love oneself is to pay homage to the divine spark that resides within each of us - a spark that kindles our potential and propels our aspirations.

Self-love serves as the bedrock upon which all other forms of love flourish. It is the fertile soil from which our relationships with others burgeon and blossom. When we love ourselves unconditionally, we create an overflowing reservoir of love that cascades into the lives of those around us. It is a ripple effect that extends far beyond the confines of our immediate sphere, igniting hearts and inspiring transformative change on a grand scale.

Self-love is akin to a tapestry intricately woven from the threads of acceptance, compassion, and forgiveness. It entails embracing the entirety of our being - the light and the shadows, the victories and the trials. It beckons us on a journey of profound self-discovery, wherein every twist and turn unveils new dimensions of our inner most selves. To love oneself is to waltz fearlessly with vulnerability, to luxuriate in the brilliance of our authenticity.

Embracing our vulnerabilities does not render us feeble; rather, it fortifies our resilience. It necessitates courage - the courage to peel back the layers of self-preservation and unveil our authentic selves to the world. Yet, in this unveiling, we unearth a strength hitherto unknown - a strength that emanates from the very core of our authenticity. It is this strength that empowers us to confront life's adversities with unwavering resolve, secure in the knowledge that we are more than sufficient, just as we are.

Within the sanctum of self-love, we discover sanctuary from the tempests of self-doubt and insecurity. It is a sacred refuge wherein our flaws cease to be perceived as weaknesses but are instead revered as badges of honor, emblematic of our shared humanity. Through the prism of self-love, we emerge as warriors of the heart - fortified with the courage to confront life's tribulations head-on. For within the depths of our own hearts, we discover the fortitude to surmount any obstacle that dares to impede our path.

Self-love is not a destination to be reached but rather an ongoing journey - an expedition of self-discovery and self-acceptance. Along this odyssey, we may stumble and falter, yet with each stumble arises the opportunity for resplendent resurgence. It is a journey that demands patience, perseverance, and, above all, a profound compassion towards oneself.

The crux of self-love lies in the tender embrace of self-compassion - the salve that soothes the wounds of self-critique. It necessitates extending grace to ourselves in moments of imperfection - acknowledging that we are all perpetual works in progress. Through the act of extending kindness to ourselves, we engender a cascade of love that permeates every facet of our existence. For within the sanctuary of self-compassion, we unearth solace amid the tempests of life.

Self-compassion transcends the notion of turning a blind eye to our flaws or imperfections; rather, it entails embracing them wholeheartedly. It entails there cognition of our shared humanity and the acknowledgment that imperfection is an inherent facet of the human condition. Through the lens of self-compassion, we foster a profound sense of inner peace and contentment.

The bloom of empowerment flourishes within the fertile grounds of self-love - taking root in the recesses of our souls and unfurling its resplendent petals in the effulgence of our authenticity. Through the act of loving ourselves fiercely, we assume the mantle of architects of our destinies - crafting lives suffused with purpose and ardor. It is a voyage of self-actualization - a journey wherein each stride forward serves as a testament to our resilience and inner fortitude.

Self-love is not synonymous with egoism or conceit; rather, it embodies the profound acknowledgment of our own worthiness- an unwavering belief that we are deserving of every blessing that graces our path. Through the act of loving ourselves, we grant ourselves permission to pursue our dreams and to traverse life's vicissitudes on our own terms.

Yet, the pathway to self-love is not invariably smooth; it is beset with obstacles and trials that test the very essence of our being. In a world replete with forces that seek to diminish our worth and devalue our contributions, it necessitates unparalleled courage to stand resolute in our truth. It entails silencing the cacophony of self-doubt and hearkening to the whispers of self-assurance that reverberate within. It is about reclaiming our sovereignty and re-scripting the narrative of our lives on our own terms.

Self-love is not contingent upon external validation or approval; rather, it emanates from a deep-seated sense of validation and approval within us. It demands the acknowledgment that we are enough, just as we are, and that our worth is not contingent upon the opinions or judgments of others. Through the act of loving ourselves unconditionally, we inoculate ourselves against the opinions of those who seek to undermine us.

As we navigate the labyrinth of existence, let us never relinquish sight of the paramount significance of self-love. It stands as a guiding beacon that illumines the path through the darkest of nights, elucidating the trajectory to our most authentic selves. Let us, therefore, love ourselves with a fervor that knows no bounds, for it is within the embrace of self-love that we unearth the fortitude to ascend to heights that transcend our most fervent aspirations. Through the act of loving ourselves, we not only empower ourselves but also galvanize women nationwide to embrace the quintessence of their own divine worth.

In loving ourselves, we emerge as luminous beacons - illuminating the path for others to traverse. We become catalysts for transformative change, inspiring others to embark upon their own odyssey of self-discovery and self-love. Thus, together, as a collective of empowered women, we ascend stronger, more radiant, and more resplendent than ever before.

2
SELF ACCEPTANCE

SELF-ACCEPTANCE

Amidst the relentless currents of life, where expectations ebb and flow like the tides, there exists an unwavering truth - the path to profound fulfillment begins with self-acceptance. This journey, oft-neglected yet paramount, invites us to shed the layers of conditioning that have obscured our authentic selves, allowing the radiant essence within to shine forth uninhibited.

From the moment we enter this world, a myriad of external voices clamor for our attention, each asserting its vision of who we ought to be. Parents, teachers, peers, societal norms - a cacophony of influences that can gradually erode our sense of self, leaving us adrift in a sea of contradictions. We contort ourselves, consciously and unconsciously, in pursuit of ideals that may not align with our intrinsic nature, all in a desperate bid for acceptance and belonging.

Yet, it is in this constant striving to meet external standards that we risk losing sight of our most authentic selves. We become strangers in our skin, disconnected from the wellspring of authenticity that resides within us. It is a paradox that plagues countless individuals, sacrificing their inherent worth upon the altar of conformity.

The journey of self-acceptance begins with a simple yet profound act of courage - the willingness to pause amidst the constant noise and turn inward with radical honesty. It is a sacred moment of reckoning, where we shed the masks we've adorned for too long and bear witness to the multifaceted tapestry of our being, flaws and all.

In this stillness, we may encounter aspects of ourselves that we've long suppressed or denied - the quirks, idiosyncrasies, and perceived imperfections that once filled us with shame or insecurity. Yet, it is in this genuine embrace that we discover the profoundest beauty, for these are the very qualities that render us gloriously human and distinctly ourselves.

To embark on this transformative path is to cultivate a relationship of profound compassion and tenderness with the self. It is to extend the same unconditional love and understanding that we so freely offer to others, turning that benevolent gaze inward. For too long, we have been our own harshest critics, berating ourselves with a level of cruelty we would never inflict upon another soul.

Self-acceptance beckons us to lay down the weapons of self-judgment and self-loathing, replacing them with a nurturing embrace that celebrates our unique tapestry. It is a radical act of defiance against a world that seeks to homogenize and diminish our individuality, a reclamation of our sovereign worth that transcends external validation.

With this newfound self-acceptance, we unlock a profoundly liberating truth - that our value is not contingent upon meeting arbitrary standards or conforming to societal molds. We come to understand that our mere existence is a miracle, a unique expression of the vast tapestry of human experience that deserves to be honored and celebrated in its entirety.

This realization ushers in a seismic shift, a profound sense of inner peace and confidence that permeates every aspect of our lives. We become more resilient in the face of life's inevitable challenges, for our worth is no longer tethered to external circumstances or the opinions of others. Instead, it is rooted in the unshakable foundation of self-acceptance, a bedrock upon which we can weather any storm.

Moreover, when we embrace our authentic selves, we open the floodgates to personal growth and fulfillment. We become more attuned to our deepest passions and purpose, allowing us to align our actions and choices with the divine spark that resides within. Paths that once seemed obscured by self-doubt and fear now reveal themselves, inviting us to step forth and explore the boundless potential that awaits when we honor our most authentic nature.

It is a journey of profound self-discovery, where we unearth the myriad facets of our identity - the talents, strengths, and gifts that have been patiently awaiting our recognition. We come to understand that our perceived flaws are often merely signposts pointing towards our unique brilliance, awaiting the discerning eye of self-acceptance to illuminate their radiance.

In this space of profound self-love, we cultivate a magnetic presence that inspired others to embark upon their journeys of self-acceptance. Our unapologetic embrace of our authentic selves becomes a beacon of hope, igniting the spark of possibility in those who have long struggled to silence the cacophony of external voices.

For it is in this collective awakening that we can truly transform the world around us. When each of us dares to shine our unique light, unencumbered by the shackles of self-doubt and self-rejection, we create a tapestry of human experience that is both breathtakingly diverse and profoundly interconnected.

Self-acceptance is not a finite destination but a perpetual odyssey - a continuous process of shedding, unfolding, and becoming. There will be moments when the tides of self-doubt rise once more when the siren call of societal expectations threatens to lure us from our path. In these moments, we must anchor ourselves in the unwavering truth of our intrinsic worth, extending the same compassion and understanding to ourselves that we so freely offer to others.

Self-acceptance is not merely a personal pursuit; it is a revolutionary act, a defiant stance against a world that seeks to commodify and diminish the boundless beauty of human existence. It is a reclamation of our sovereignty, a declaration that we will no longer abandon ourselves in pursuit of ideals that do not resonate with our most profound truth.

So, let us embark upon this odyssey together, hand in hand, bearing witness to one another's magnificence. Let us shed the shrouds of self-doubt and embrace the breathtaking tapestry of our individuality, weaving a collective narrative of radical self-love that transcends generations.

In this sacred space, we will discover that the path to genuine fulfillment and joy does not lie in the relentless pursuit of external validation but in the profound act of accepting ourselves - in all our messy, glorious, and unapologetically human splendor.

THE MAGIC OF SELF ACCEPTANCE

The next phase is Self-Acceptance. This feels like peace. Self-acceptance is where you allow yourself to be who you are. Instead of running, changing, or trying to fix, you surrender to what is.

Self-Acceptance

Life is too brief to dwell on the negative aspects of oneself. A positive side effect of her obesity, she said, was that she was well-liked by friends and family, who appreciated her kind, cuddly embrace. So, she said, society and culture put a lot of pressure on individuals, even while science says one thing, then changes its mind in a few months or years on the link between body weight and health. Being overweight is not a problem until you want to make it a problem. We all want to live long, healthy lives filled with wise decisions, but this can' happen until we first change our thinking. The most important thing to remember is to treat oneself with kindness and respect. She revealed to me the following: Loving yourself has nothing to do with how you look or your size.

As a result, those who have a high level of self-acceptance are better able to handle criticism. They know it's appropriate to accept and love oneself while simultaneously striving to better oneself on a regular basis. But what does it mean to accept oneself as one is? And why are some individuals more self-confident than others? When it comes to cultivating more of this quality, what are the best practices? Let us investigate this further.

What does it mean to accept oneself?

In order to practice self-acceptance, you must come to terms with and embrace your own nature, flaws and all. Whether they're good or bad, you've got to deal with them. This encompasses both your physical and psychological characteristics.

Self-acceptance involves acknowledging that your worth extends beyond the sum total of your unique traits and behaviors. Self-acceptance is also referred to as extreme self-acceptance. Having a positive self-perception helps you to be more resilient in the face of criticism. It implies a complete and absolute acceptance of one's whole self, good or bad. To acquire self acceptance, you must learn to embrace the elements of yourself that you deem unattractive or unappealing. Acknowledging and celebrating your strengths and accomplishments is just as crucial. Keeping track of your objectives and how far you've come is a great way to identify your talents.

This is why so many of us have difficulty accepting ourselves. Hidden, neglected, and rejected elements of ourselves are often hidden, ignored, and rejected. It is preferable to alter things than accept them. Despite the fact that it seems paradoxical, accepting all of our flaws might actually motivate us to work on the ones we dislike the most. It is a hallmark of emotional intelligence to be conscious of one's own limits as a starting point for personal progress.

Self-acceptance is more than just admitting our flaws and giving up on trying to improve upon them. On the other hand, it implies being aware of our flaws but without any emotional relationship to them. When we become more self-aware, we may make positive changes to our routines and our behavior.

Is it easier to get through the day when you embrace who you are?
According to studies, a person's total mental health and well-being depend heavily on their ability to accept themselves. There seems to be a clear relationship between poor self-acceptance and mental

illness, according to the data. As you can see, there are many ways in which poor self-acceptance impacts your everyday activities (such as your career, relationships, and well-being) as well. For instance, consider the following five instances:

1. Self-acceptance Helps You Regulate Your Emotions

Having low self-esteem might have a negative impact on the area of your brain that governs your emotions. Mental imbalance and emotional outbursts might come from increased worry, tension, or rage as a consequence of these feelings.

You can't be happy if you don't accept who you are. Mental and emotional well-being is also affected. In doing so, it keeps you focused on the bad qualities of yourself, which in turn generates unpleasant feelings towards you.

Self-acceptance, on the other hand, has been shown to be associated with higher levels of happiness and well-being. When you embrace your flaws, you may feel better about yourself and lessen the impact of stress and despair on your body.

2. Self-Acceptance Helps in Forgiving Oneself

Less self-criticism comes from accepting who you are. As a result, you're able to cultivate a more empathetic, sympathetic, and objective sense of your own worth.

One doctor at Harvard Medical School believes that acceptance and forgiveness are inseparable. He claims that our incapacity to accept and forgive ourselves leads us to divide into several sections.

The desire to forgive and the need to be forgiven are diametrically opposed in nature. Self-acceptance may help you bridge the distance between them, allowing you to forgive yourself for your errors and move on.

Concentrating on the past can trap you in a loop of negative thoughts and feelings, and this is vital for your well-being.

3. Self-Acceptance Boosts Your Self-Esteem

- As a result of self-acceptance, you'll feel more confident in your abilities. Your apparent flaws are not what makes you who you are or what you're worth.
- With confidence, it is easier to take action even when you are afraid. A lack of self-acceptance, on the other hand, might prevent you from pursuing your ambitions.
- When you embrace your flaws, you know that failure does not define you and is only a chance to grow.
- Your self-confidence might also provide you with more freedom. It gives you the freedom to make choices on your own, independent of the opinions of others.

4. Self-Acceptance Leads to Compassion for Oneself

In the words of Kristin Neff, a self-compassion researcher, self-compassion is more essential than self-esteem for our mental and emotional well-being

"The same warmth and care you would offer to a close friend" is what she means when she says that you should practice self-compassion. If you are struggling to accept yourself, you know that you're your own greatest enemy.

Developing self-compassion might help you be more forgiving of yourself when things go wrong and help you bounce back from setbacks.

5. Self-Acceptance Lets You Be Who You Really Are

Lack of self-acceptance, leads to a life of self-censorship and self-repression. There is a chance that this could leave one exhausted.

The ability to accept oneself is and not worry about what other people think of them may help them present themselves more truthfully. To put it simply: When one accepts themselves, they feel free to be who they are.

Please take a few moments to reflect on the things that offer you joy. No, I don't think so. Cook yourself a dinner from a new cookbook, if you'd like. Are you a creative person? Consider getting out your paints and creating more art or enrolling in a class. Your vision board may have several images of exotic locales. After that, begin planning your next vacation and put money aside to make it happen. Love is all about making each other happy. Pleasure is an element of each connection that develops, whether it's romantic or otherwise. Their passion is free of guile if they allow themselves to be fully immersed in it.

The more pleasure they pursue, the more happiness they experience, and the more happiness they experience, the more accepted they feel. They'll come to understand the significance of their existence. Their perspective on life changed. An important part of achieving self-acceptance was trusting and accepting their own instincts. As a kid, there were times when their mother would tell them that the needed to go to the gym and eat healthy food. Some days they're a salad eater and a workout junkie, while other days, they're both. It's okay to refuse to put on clothes on certain days as they eat cupcakes.

 It's a concept known as "balance". A well-lived life requires an understanding of the importance of maintaining a sense of equilibrium. They stopped feeling awful about themselves when they ate cupcakes or other meals that the rest of the world considered unhealthy for them. They started to examine their primal desires and caved in. A few bites of a gourmet cupcake are all they need to feel full for the rest of the day. In the past, they would have eaten it all out of humiliation. Not anymore.

They automatically sought less food after removing the guilt and humiliation associated with overeating. Getting in touch with their own aspirations might help alleviate feelings of guilt. In so far as they may regard them as their own identifiers for a fulfilled existence, being able to accept oneself is much simpler when they have greater faith in themselves. Allowing ourselves to be who we really are means respecting our innate instincts. We respect our own truth. By recognizing our genuine selves, we are able to completely express ourselves.

A STORY OF STRENGTH AND RESILIENCE: LEARNING TO WALK ALONE

I grew up dreaming of a mother-daughter relationship that would be as cozy as a warm blanket on a cold night. I wanted a mom who'd be there with me through all the ups and downs, someone who'd make me feel like I was the most important person in the world. I pictured us having deep conversations, laughing together, and sharing life's little moments.

I imagined her being proud of me no matter what I did, cheering me on from the sidelines, and helping me pick up the pieces when Life got tough.

But reality is often much harsher than our dreams, and my relationship with my mom was no exception. Instead of warmth and affection, I was met with harsh words and a cold shoulder. Instead of support, I was greeted with criticism and judgment. It was as if I was always walking on eggshells, waiting for the next negative comment or disapproving look.

One of the earliest memories I have of this disconnect was when I scraped my knee. I was little, and I remember running to my mom, hoping for a comforting hug and a few kind words to make it all better. But instead of soothing me, she told me to stop crying because it was "just a scratch." I felt dismissed, like my pain didn't matter. It made me believe that my emotions weren't valid, that expressing my feelings was a sign of weakness.

As I grew older, this pattern of emotional neglect continued. I tried so hard to get her attention and approvals, thinking that if I could just be perfect, she'd finally see me. I worked my heart out in school, dreaming that maybe she'd be proud of me if I excelled. But even when I graduated from university- her only child to earn a degree she didn't come to my graduation. I was devastated. Here I was, achieving something huge, and she didn't even care enough to show up. Her absence that day told me everything I needed to know about where I stood in her life.

The constant negativity and lack of support took a toll on me. I started second-guessing myself, wondering if I was doing something wrong or if I was the problem. I spent so much energy trying to prove my worth, hoping she'd notice me and give me the validation I craved. But it never came. It was exhausting and left me feeling empty, like I was never good enough.

Eventually, I realized I had to make a choice. I couldn't keep seeking approval from someone who was incapable of giving it. It was like trying to squeeze water from a stone-it just wasn't going to happen. I knew I needed to take control of my life and create boundaries to protect my health a constant source of comfort and guidance. It was the hardest decision I've ever made, but it was also incredibly freeing.

Walking away from my mother wasn't easy. Despite everything, she was still my mom. But I knew I deserved better deserved love, respect, and understanding, all things she couldn't give me. I started focusing on building relationships with people who valued me for who I was. I found joy in my accomplishments, even if she never acknowledged them.

It was a new beginning, a chance to live my life on my own terms.

 A healthy mother-daughter relationship is built on mutual respect and support. It's a bond where the mother encourages her daughter to grow, offers guidance, and is a source of comfort. A mother should be someone who listens without judgment and makes you feel safe. But my mother never played that role. Instead, she favored my siblings and left me feeling isolated. My efforts to earn her approval were fruitless, and her behavior wasn't just emotionally abusive-it was sometimes physically abusive, too.

There were moments when her anger was so intense that I felt scared and unsafe in my own home. I knew I couldn't continue living this way. I needed to break the cycle of abuse, to step away and create a life where I could be at peace. It was a turning point, a moment when I realized I needed to prioritize my well-being over my desire for her approval.

Navigating the transition from childhood to adulthood can be a complex journey for both mothers and daughters. As daughters grow into adults, it's crucial for mothers to adjust their approach to reflect their daughter's newfound independence and maturity. Treating an adult daughter like a young child can lead to frustration and hinder the growth of their relationship. To foster a healthy bond, mothers need to respect their daughters' autonomy and recognize that they are now capable of making their own decisions.

One key to successful mother-daughter relationships is open communication. Mothers should listen without judgment and offer guidance rather than impose their views. This approach allows daughters to feel valued and respected, reinforcing their confidence as they navigate adult life.

Additionally, mothers should embrace their daughters' achievements without jealousy. It can be challenging to see a daughter excel in arcs where a mother may have faced obstacles. However, it's vital to celebrate these successes, acknowledging that a daughter's accomplishments do not diminish a mother's own worth. Instead, they reflect the positive influence and support a mother has provided over the years.

By understanding these dynamics, mothers can build a stronger, more harmonious relationship with their daughters, rooted in mutual respect and genuine support.

If you find yourself in a similar situation, know that it's okay to set boundaries. You don't have to tolerate abuse or disrespect, even from family. Sometimes, creating distance is the best thing you can do for your mental and emotional health. It might feel like you're losing something important but your peace of mind is worth it.

Motherly love is Unique and profound bond that transcends age, culture and circumstances. Despite the inevitable passage of the time, the essence of a mother's love remains a constant source of comfort and guidance. No matter how old a child may become, the need for that nurturing touch, compassionate ear, and gentle reassurance is timeless. This yearning is deeply rooted in our human experience, echoing the bond formed during infancy when a mother's embrace provided safety and warmth.

As children grow into adults, the dynamics of the relationship may change, but the emotional foundation laid by a mother's love persists. It becomes a symbol of stability in a world that can often seem unpredictable. Seeking a mother's guidance, even in adulthood, is not a sign of weakness but rather an acknowledgment of the special connection that can weather any storm. It's the recognition that, at any stage of life, there's someone who truly understands and unconditionally accepts us.

There's nothing wrong with this yearning. It is a testament to the enduring power of a mother's love and the human need for connection. Society often pressures us to "grow up" and leave behind such dependencies, but emotional bonds like these are not a burden; they are a source of strength and resilience. Embracing this yearning is to honor the profound impact a mother's love has on shaping who we are.

As I began to heal, I stumbled upon a powerful analogy that helped me make sense of my situation. In a conversation between Oprah Winfrey and T.D. Jakes, Oprah asked why her birth mother couldn't give her the love she needed. T.D. Jakes responded with a metaphor that made everything click: "You're a gallon. Your mother was a pint. She could only pour what she had, but it was never going to fill you up." It hit me like a ton of bricks my mother simply didn't have the capacity to give me the love and support I needed. It wasn't my fault, and it wasn't because I wasn't good enough. She just didn't have it in her.

Understanding this allowed me to let go of the need for her approval and focus on what truly mattered: my happiness and well-being. I started surrounding myself with people who genuinely cared about me, who celebrated my successes, and who provided the emotional support I always longed for. It made all the difference in the world.

If you're dealing with a toxic relationship with a parent, remember that you deserve love, respect, and understanding. Don't let anyone make you feel small or unworthy. Setting boundaries isn't about shutting people out -it's about creating a safe space where you can grow and thrive. Sometimes, mothers need to understand that treating an adult daughter differently from a child is crucial. They should also avoid jealousy over their daughter's achievements and instead celebrate them.

I know how hard it can be to walk away from toxic relationships, especially when they involve family. It feels like you're breaking something sacred, like you're letting go of something that should be unbreakable. But I want you to know that it's okay to choose yourself. I's okay to put your needs first. Your mental health is precious, and you have every right to protect it. Sometimes, that means stepping away from people who bring you down, who belittle you, or who make you doubt your own worth.

Most importantly, love yourself. Believe in your worth, and never let anyone dim your light. You deserve happiness, success, and the kind of love that fills a gallon and then some.

So take a deep breath, trust your instincts, and step boldly into your future. You've got this.

I believe in you, and you should believe in yourself too.

EMBRACING THE JOURNEY TO BEING COMFORTABLE IN YOUR OWN SKIN

In a world filled with societal pressures and constantly shifting ideals of beauty, finding comfort in your own skin can be challenging. Yet, embracing authenticity and developing self-acceptance are fundamental to leading a fulfilling and meaningful life. This journey isn't about meeting external expectations; it's about embracing who you are, imperfections and all. In this essay, we'll explore the process of finding comfort in your own skin, the challenges we face, and the profound impact it can have on our well-being.

THE WEIGHT OF SOCIETAL EXPECTATIONS

From an early age, we're bombarded with images and messages that shape our perception of beauty, success, and worth. Advertising, social media, and entertainment industries often portray a narrow definition of what it means to be attractive or successful. These portrayals can create unrealistic standards that many people feel pressured to meet. The result is a constant comparison to others, leading to feelings of inadequacy and insecurity.

Consider the rise of social media platforms like Instagram, where influencers and celebrities curate idealized versions of their lives. The carefully edited photos and highlight reels can make it seem like everyone else has it all figured out, leading to a sense of not measuring up. The pressure to conform to these ideals can be overwhelming, pushing individuals to engage in extreme diets, excessive exercise, or even cosmetic procedures.

THE POWER OF SELF-ACCEPTANCE

Amidst this whirlwind of societal expectations, self-acceptance emerges as a powerful counterbalance. It involves recognizing your unique qualities and accepting them without judgment. Self-acceptance isn't about becoming complacent; rather, it's about acknowledging your strengths and weaknesses while striving for personal growth.

To be comfortable in your own skin, you must first understand your values and belief. This involves introspection and reflection, asking yourself questions like: "What do I truly care about?" and "What makes me feel alive?" By connecting with your core values, you can begin to build a sense of identity that is independent of external influences.

One crucial step in the journey to self-acceptance is embracing vulnerability. Brene Brown, a renowned researcher on vulnerability and shame, emphasizes the importance of allowing yourself to be seen and heard, even when it's uncomfortable. By sharing your authentic self with others, you create meaningful connections and build deeper relationships.

Vulnerability allows you to break free from the armor of perfection and experience genuine human connection.

OVERCOMING NEGATIVE SELF-TALK

Negative self-talk is a common obstacle on the path to self-acceptance. It's the inner critic that constantly points out flaws and mistakes, often magnifying them to the point of self-sabotage. To overcome negative self-talk, it's essential to challenge these thoughts and replace them with positive affirmations.

Consider the impact of reframing negative thoughts into positive ones. Instead of thinking, "Im not good enough," try saying, "I am enough just as I am." This shift in mindset can have a profound effect on your confidence and overall sense of self-worth. It takes practice and consistency, but over time, these positive affirmations become a natural part of your internal dialogue.

THE ONGOING JOURNEY OF SELF-DISCOVERY

Finding comfort in your own skin is an ongoing journey, not a destination. It requires patience, self-compassion, and a willingness to embrace change. As you continue to grow and evolve, your understanding of yourself will deepen, and your comfort in your own skin will naturally increase.

Remember that everyone's journey is unique. There is no one-size-fits-all approach to self-acceptance. Embrace your individuality and honor your personal journey. Celebrate your progress, no matter how small, and recognize that setbacks are a natural part of growth.

IN CONCLUSION

Being comfortable in your own skin is about embracing authenticity, challenging negative self-talk, and finding support in a compassionate community. It's a journey of self-discovery and personal growth that leads to a more fulfilling and meaningful life. By embracing who you are, you open the door to a world of possibilities and create the foundation for lasting happiness.

EMBRACING YOUR WORTH: A GUIDE TO SELF-VALUE AND EMPOWERMENT FOR WOMEN

INTRODUCTION: EMBRACING YOUR INHERENT WORTH

In a world where societal standards often attempt to define a woman's worth by superficial measures, it's imperative for every woman to reclaim her power and acknowledge her intrinsic value. Your worth transcends the confines of external validation - it's deeply rooted in your essence, your strength, and your unyielding spirit.

As you embark on this journey of self-discovery and self-love, remember that you are enough - just as you are. Embrace your flaws, celebrate your victories, and honor the woman you are becoming. You possess an innate strength and resilience that can weather any storm and conquer any obstacle.

So, stand tall, dear woman, and let your light shine bright. Your worth is immeasurable, your potential limitless, and your journey one of endless possibilities. Embrace the power within you, and watch as the world transforms in response to your authenticity and your grace. You are unstoppable.

UNDERSTANDING YOUR VALUE: SELF-REFLECTION AND AWARENESS

In a world where women are often subjected to societal expectations and stereotypes, it's crucial to take a moment to reflect on our own inherent value and strength. Empowerment starts from within, and self-Inspection is the key to unlocking our full potential.

When we pause to truly understand our value, we begin to recognize the unique qualities and abilities that make us who we are. It's about acknowledging our strengths, talents, and accomplishments, no matter how big or small they may seem. Each of us has a story to tell, experiences to share, and lessons learned along the way.

Self-awareness plays a vital role in this journey of empowerment. By tuning into our thoughts, emotions, and desires, we gain clarity about what truly matters to us. We become attuned to our needs and aspirations, allowing us to set meaningful goals and pursue them with conviction.

It's important to remember that self-worth isn't dependent on external validation. We don't need the approval of others to recognize our value. True empowerment comes from within, from a deep sense of self-assurance and confidence in our abilities.

As women, we often face societal pressures to conform to certain standards of beauty, success, and behavior. But true empowerment means breaking free from these constraints and embracing our authentic selves. It's about celebrating our differences and owning our uniqueness with pride.

Self-reflection also involves examining our beliefs and attitudes about ourselves and the world around us. It requires us to challenge limiting beliefs and replace them with empowering ones. Instead of doubting ourselves, we learn to trust in our abilities and embrace new opportunities with courage and resilience.

By cultivating self-awareness and understanding our value, we become unstoppable forces of change. We no longer shy away from challenges but instead, embrace them as opportunities for growth and self-discovery. We refuse to let fear hold us back and step into our power with confidence and determination.

Empowerment isn't just about empowering ourselves; it's also about lifting up other women along the way. By supporting and uplifting one another, we create a ripple effect of positive change that extends far beyond ourselves. Together, we can break down barriers, challenge stereotypes, and pave the way for a more inclusive and equitable future.

NURTURING SELF-RESPECT: SETTING BOUNDARIES AND PRIORITIZING SELF-CARE

Self-respect serves as the cornerstone of self-worth, forming the bedrock upon which our empowerment flourishes. It commences with the firm establishment of boundaries that unapologetically uphold our needs, values, and overall well-being. Embrace the power of "no" when confronted with situations that erode your energy or compromise your integrity. Assertively decline anything that detracts from your essence, for in doing so, you reclaim your autonomy and direct your path towards empowerment.

Central to this journey is the unwavering commitment to self-care practices that nurture every facet of your being-mind, body, and spirit. Cultivate a sanctuary of self-love by integrating mindfulness exercises, regular physical activity, and indulgence in hobbies that ignite your passion. Prioritize these rituals as sacred obligations, for they serve as the cornerstone of your resilience and vitality.

Embrace the philosophy that you cannot pour from an empty cup. By steadfastly prioritizing your own well-being, you replenish your inner reservoirs, empowering you to radiate your fullest potential in every facet of your life. Within the sanctity of self-care lies the transformative power to transcend limitations and manifest your most authentic self.

In honoring your own needs and boundaries, you pave the path to unbridled empowerment. Reject the notion of self-sacrifice as a badge of honor; instead, view prioritizing yourself as an act of radical self-love and empowerment. As you unapologetically advocate for your own needs, you dismantle antiquated paradigms of female selflessness and embrace the revolutionary concept of self-possession.

Each assertion of your boundaries becomes a declaration of your inherent worth, resonating with the fierce clarity of a woman who refuses to diminish per light for the comfort of others. Through your unwavering commitment to self-respect, you inspire those around you to honor their own truth and forge their unique path towards empowerment.

Embrace the potency of your voice, for it holds the power to reshape narratives and ignite revolutions. Stand tall in your authenticity, for therein lies your true strength. As you navigate the intricate tapestry of life, let the compass of self-respect guide your every decision, empowering you to embrace your worth and create s legacy of unyielding empowerment for generations to come.

OWNING YOUR STRENGTHS: CELEBRATING YOUR UNIQUE QUALITIES

Every woman holds within herself a remarkable blend of strengths, talents, and qualities that distinguish her from anyone else. Rather than measuring ourselves against others, let's revel in what sets us apart. It's time to stand tall and acknowledge our achievements, regardless of their scale. Whether it's our boundless creativity, unwavering resilience, profound compassion, or razor-sharp intelligence, let's celebrate these attributes and allow them to radiate with brilliance.

Let's embark on the exhilarating journey of self-discovery and personal growth. Let's dive into uncharted territories, exploring new skills, passions, and avenues for development. Always bear in mind that our potential knows no bounds. Every obstacle we conquer, every setback we overcome, only serves to fortify our inner strength and resilience.

As women, we possess an inherent ability to navigate the complexities of life with grace and determination. We are architects of change, pioneers of progress, and champions of our own destinies. Our voices are powerful, our actions impactful. Let's seize every opportunity to make our mark on the world, to leave a legacy of empowerment and inspiration for generations to come.

Embrace your individuality, for therein lies your greatest strength. Embrace your flaws, for they are the building blocks of your resilience. Embrace your dreams, for they hold the key to your future. And above all, embrace your power, for it is the catalyst for change and the driving force behind your success.

In a world that often seeks to diminish our worth and limit our potential, let us stand firm in our convictions and unapologetically embrace our greatness. Let us support and uplift one another, recognizing that our collective strength knows no bounds. Together, we can shatter glass ceilings, defy expectations, and rewrite the narrative of what it means to be a woman in today's world.

So, my fellow women, I urge you to embrace your power, your potential, and your purpose. Dare to dream big, dare to pursue your passions, and dare to be unapologetically yourself. For in doing so, you not only empower yourself but also inspire others to do the same. The world is waiting for you to unleash your greatness-so go forth and conquer it with unwavering confidence and determination.

OVERCOMING SELF-DOUBT: CULTIVATING CONFIDENCE AND RESILIENCE

In the journey of self-empowerment, self-doubt often lurks as a formidable barrier. Yet, it's crucial to understand that confidence isn't about banishing doubt entirely; it's about confronting it head-on and forging ahead regardless .As women, we possess an innate strength to challenge, evolve, and thrive.

Banish the notion that confidence means never feeling uncertain. Instead, recognize that it's the courage to embrace uncertainty and still stride forward with purpose. Reframe negative self-talk into affirmations of your capabilities and worth. Remind yourself daily of your strengths and the value you bring to every situation.

Setting realistic goals is another cornerstone of empowerment. Breakdown your aspirations into manageable steps, allowing yourself to progress steadily. Each achievement, no matter how small, is a testament to your resilience and determination. Celebrate these victories wholeheartedly, fueling your motivation to conquer new challenges.

Failure is not a verdict on your abilities; it's a stepping stone toward growth and self-discovery. Embrace setbacks as opportunities to glean invaluable insights and refine your approach. Learn from each experience, emerging stronger and more resilient than before. Understand that setbacks do not define you; your response to them does.

Surround yourself with a tribe of empowered women who champion your ambitions and celebrate your successes. Seek out mentors and role models who inspire you to reach higher and push beyond perceived limitations. Share your journey with those who uplift and encourage you, fostering a supportive network that fuels your aspirations.

Above all, trust in your inherent power and potential. You are capable of achieving greatness beyond measure. Embrace your uniqueness, stand tall in your convictions, and fearlessly pursue your dreams. Remember, your journey to empowerment is not a solo endeavor, it's a collective movement of women empowering women. Together, we rise, unstoppable and unapologetic in our pursuit of greatness.

REJECTING EXTERNAL VALIDATION: FINDING VALIDATION WITHIN

In a society that often dictates what a woman should look like, how she should behave, and what she should aspire to, it's crucial for women to reclaim their power by recognizing the inherent value within themselves. Instead of constantly seeking external validation, it's time to turn inward and acknowledge our worth independent of others' opinions.

Embracing self-compassion and self-acceptance is the first step towards empowerment. We must understand that we are inherently deserving of love, respect, and validation simply because we exist as individuals. Our worth is not contingent upon the approval of others; it is an intrinsic aspect of our being.

Cultivating a mindset of gratitude for our unique qualities and life experiences is essential. Rather than comparing ourselves to unrealistic standards set by society, we should celebrate our individuality and the journey that has shaped us into who we are today. By embracing our authenticity and owning our stories, we empower ourselves to live fully and unapologetically.

When we validate ourselves from within, we become immune to the external pressures and judgments that often hold us back. We no longer seek validation from others because we understand that our worth cannot be determined by their perceptions. Instead, we trust in our own intuition and inner wisdom to guide us on our path.

Empowerment comes from standing firmly in our truth and refusing to conform to societal expectations. It's about embracing our flaws and imperfections as integral parts of our identity. By honoring our true selves and living authentically, we inspire others to do the same.

In a world that may try to diminish our worth, let us rise above the noise and affirm our value with unwavering confidence. Let us celebrate our strength, resilience, and inherent worthiness as women. Together, we can redefine what it means to be empowered and pave the way for future generations of women to do the same.

FOSTERING HEALTHY RELATIONSHIPS: SURROUNDING YOURSELF WITH SUPPORT

In a world where women often face societal pressures and expectations, the relationships we foster become crucial pillars of our empowerment and self-worth. Every interaction, every connection, holds the potential to either uplift or diminish us. Therefore, it's imperative to curate a circle of individuals who not only recognize but celebrate our strengths, ambitions, and unique qualities.

Empowerment stems from the bonds we form with others - those who see our potential and actively encourage us to reach for the stars. Surround yourself with friends, mentors, and partners who champion your dreams, who stand beside you through every challenge, and who applaud your victories with genuine joy. These are the relationships that fuel our confidence, enabling us to stride boldly towards our aspirations, unencumbered by doubt or hesitation.

Yet, alongside fostering positive connections, we must also recognize the importance of setting boundaries with those who seek to undermine or diminish our worth. Toxic individuals, whether intentional or not, can sap our energy and erode our self-esteem. Asserting boundaries isn't an act of selfishness; rather, it's an act of self-preservation and empowerment. By safeguarding our emotional well-being, we reclaim control over our lives, refusing to allow negativity to detract from our sense of worth.

Indeed, we owe it to ourselves to invest in relationships that nurture our souls and inspire us to grow. Authenticity and trust form the bedrock of such connections, allowing us to express ourselves freely, without fear of judgment or rejection. It's within these safe havens of acceptance that we find the courage to explore our passions, Chase our ambitions, and embrace our true selves without reservation.

So, dear women, know this: you are deserving of love, respect, and support in all your relationships. Your worth is inherent, immutable, and not contingent upon the opinions of others. Embrace the power within you to cultivate a tribe that lifts you higher, that celebrates your journey, and that empowers you to live unapologetically. For in the company of those who see your light and honor your essence, you will shine brighter than ever before, illuminating the path for others to follow in your wake.

PURSUING YOUR PASSIONS: UNLEASHING YOUR POTENTIAL AND AMBITION

Embrace your passions and let them ignite the fire within you to conquer the world. Your ambitions are not mere wishes; they are the blueprints of your destiny. Embrace them fiercely, for they are the compass guiding you towards the life you envision. Whether your heart yearns for entrepreneurship, academic pursuits, or social change, dare to chase after your dreams with unwavering determination.

In the face of uncertainty, stand tall and resolute. Fear and self-doubt may whisper tales of inadequacy, but you are a force to be reckoned with. Refuse to be confined by the limitations of doubt. Instead, let outage be your armor and resilience your shield. Know that within you lies the power to transcend every obstacle and emerge victorious.

As a woman, you wield a strength that is both fierce and gentle, are silence that knows no bounds. Your voice has the power to spark revolutions, your actions the potential to shape destinies. Never underestimate the influence you hold, for you are a beacon of empowerment lighting the path for generations to come.

In a world that often seeks to silence your voice, rise unapologetically and claim your rightful place. Your dreams are not just yours alone; they are a testament to the courage of every woman who dared to defy the status quo. So, stand tall, speak boldly, and let the world witness the unstoppable force that you ate.

Remember, your passions are not just fleeting desires; they are the very essence of your being. Nurture them, cultivate them, and watch as they blossom into a reality beyond your wildest dreams. You are the architect of your destiny, the master of your fate. So, go forth, fearless and unyielding, and make your mark upon the world.

EMBRACING IMPERFECTION: LIBERATING YOURSELF FROM UNREALISTIC STANDARDS

In today's world, women face countless pressures to meet society's standards of perfection. From flawless appearance to impeccable performance in every aspect of life, the expectations can feel suffocating. But let me tell you something; perfection is a myth. It's an unattainable goal that only serves to make us feel inadequate and unworthy.

Instead of striving for an impossible ideal, we must embrace our flaws, quirks, and imperfections. These are the very things that make us beautifully unique. Our imperfections are not weaknesses; they are badges of honor that testify to our resilience and strength. They are reminders that we are real, authentic, and human.

But embracing imperfection isn't just about self-acceptance; it's also about self-empowerment. When we stop striving for an unattainable and instead embrace our authentic selves, we free ourselves from the shackles of society's expectations. We reclaim our power and our autonomy. We become the authors of our own stories, defining success on our own terms.

So, the next time you find yourself doubting your worth or questioning your abilities, remember this: you are enough, just as you are. You don't need to be perfect to be worthy of love and acceptance. Embrace your imperfections, for they are what make you beautifully human.

In a world that often tries to tear us down and make us feel small, embracing imperfection is an act of defiance. It's a declaration of self-love and self-worth. So, let your imperfections shine, and watch as you blossom into the powerful, empowered woman you were always meant to be.

ADVOCATING FOR YOURSELF: ASSERTIVENESS AND SELF-ADVOCACY

Advocating for yourself is not just a skill; it's a declaration of your inherent power as a woman. It's about boldly asserting your needs, desires, and boundaries in every facet of your life. Whether you're navigating the boardroom, nurturing relationships, or mingling in social circles, it's time to seize control and advocate for yourself with unapologetic certainty.

Silence is not an option. Stand tall and vocalize your worth. You are worthy of respect and dignity in every interaction, every exchange, every moment. Don't hesitate to employ assertiveness techniques, such as wielding "I" statements with conviction, drawing clear boundaries, and asserting yourself when circumstances demand it. Your voice is not just valuable; it's indispensable.

In the workplace, advocate for the recognition and compensation you rightfully deserve. Don't shrink yourself to fit into predefined roles or expectations. Speak up for your ideas, your contributions, and your ambitions. Embrace your brilliance and refuse to settle for anything less than what you're worth.

In relationships, be unyielding in your pursuit of mutual respect and understanding. Demand reciprocity and refuse to accept anything less than genuine appreciation for who you are. Set boundaries that honor your emotional well-being and uphold them steadfastly. Remember, you are not obligated to diminish yourself for the comfort of others.

Above all, recognize that you are your most powerful advocate. Your voice carries the resonance of generations of women who fought for the right to be seen and heard.

THE MAGIC OF SELF-TRUST

Practicing self-care and self-compassion leads to greater confidence in one's abilities. Self-doubt lies at the heart of many people's discontent. There are countless individuals who struggle with trust in themselves or in life. However, nurturing oneself and practicing kindness fosters a natural progression towards self-trust. Believing in oneself involves recognizing personal worth and valuing one's capabilities. Self-belief encompasses faith in one's dreams and objectives. As the journey of self-love progresses and one consistently shows up for oneself, aspirations begin to resonate more strongly and compellingly.

The More They Loved Themselves, The Easier It Was to Say Yes to Their Dreams

A long-held ambition came true while working on this book: the goal to travel and work in a different country for six months. This dream followed a departure from the corporate sector years earlier, fueled by the hope of being able to work from anywhere globally. This led to a period of indifference and disinterest in daily activities. Despite dreaming of a lifestyle that combined work and play globally, there was a sense of being stuck in area, working from a home office. However, embracing self-love reignited the ability to dream, and trusting in themselves underscored the transformative potential of dreams in leading to a fulfilling life. Believing in oneself is a declaration of self-worth. "Confidence is the fuel that propels people forward," asserts Richard Petty from Ohio State University.

After a six-year hiatus focused on raising two children, returning to the workplace was met with severe anxiety. Establishing a consulting business in2012, following the completion of a second degree and the research and writing of A World of Difference, was hindered by a crippling lack of confidence. To manage the anxiety while maintaining productivity, carefully planned work schedule was necessary, but it was clear that operating under such stress was not sustainable. The anxiety impacted performance, limited the capacity for work due to emotional and physical exhaustion, and adversely affected health. Faced with the choice. Of succumbing to fear or overcoming it, especially when it came to writing and researching A World of Difference, giving up was not an option. Instead, extensive research and experimentation were conducted on ways to enhance self-esteem. These strategies successfully countered the fear and self-limiting beliefs that had hindered reaching their full potential.

This chapter will detail the transition from a state of paralyzing fear to adopting a" feel the fear and do it anyway" attitude through proven self-confidence-building methods. These techniques are shared with the hope of aiding others who face self-doubt in realizing their own vast potential.

Developing Your Self-Confidence Techniques

Self-efficacy and minimal fear of failure are two characteristics of people with high levels of confidence. When someone believes that they are capable of accomplishing their goals, this is known as self-efficacy. People who have a low fear of failing are more likely to take risks. Self-confidence techniques might target either the self-efficacy issue or the fear of failure.

Combating Limiting Beliefs in Oneself

Many women have self-limiting attitudes that hinder them from taking the next step ahead.

When it comes to self-esteem, expectations for the future, and self-confidence, females have a lower level of self-esteem and self-confidence than males. In order to improve our self-esteem and self-confidence, we must confront and replace negative self-narratives (such as "I am not good enough, clever enough, and attractive enough") with more positive and compassionate ones.

There are three stages to rewriting your inner story and confronting yourself-limiting beliefs: Make a list of all of your self-limiting beliefs.

It's possible that some of you are already aware of your own personal misgivings and anxieties. In order to identify the ideas that are keeping you from taking action, some of you may need to go a little deeper. You may identify your self-limiting beliefs by keeping a close eye on your emotional responses. If you experience anxiety or fear in certain circumstances, you may want to take some time to examine your underlying beliefs. Observing your thoughts and feelings during the course of a typical workday might help you identify and express your self-limiting beliefs. Notice whether you minimize your accomplishments or if you credit your triumphs on others or chance. You should also be aware of any comparisons you make to other people. To be fair, we tend to focus on what others have done well rather than what they are going through within. We obsess over our flaws and overlook our accomplishments.

Your self-limiting beliefs should be challenged

Self-limiting beliefs, such as doubting one's own abilities or undervaluing one's accomplishments because of others, should be confronted by looking for evidence to the contrary. Seek the evidence that refutes your stifling self-belief. If you're having trouble doing this, pretend you're advising a buddy on how to confront their own self-limiting beliefs to help you separate yourself from your own. Describe your strategy for getting them to stop their self-defeating thoughts and start thinking positively instead. Then, use this advice in your own scenario.

It's time to rewrite the script. Replace your self-limiting ideas with sensible, reasonable, and hopeful narratives in the third phase.

Be Proud of What You've Done

Studies have shown that women are more likely than males to attribute their achievements to luck or the actions of others. Men, on the other hand, appear to attribute their success solely to their own work and abilities. A lack of self-confidence is caused by blaming others for your accomplishments.

What is it about women that makes them behave in such a way? Some people think that women are afraid of being seen as immodest, competitive, or arrogant because they are afraid of contradicting traditional feminine norms. In order to gain the trust of other females, girls learn to downplay their accomplishments.

Owning your accomplishments has a cultural component to it as well. Modesty is an essential social trait for people in African, Asian, and Middle Eastern cultures who believe in communal living. Members of such cultures are taught to minimize their personal accomplishments and instead give credit to others for their achievements.

Work on recognizing your accomplishments by keeping track of a few "highlight moments" from your time in school, work, and other endeavors. Notate in writing how each accomplishment was made possible by the organization's own internal resources and skills.

Remember your list of accomplishments when you're feeling down about yourself.

Keep Your Mistakes to Yourself

When it comes to failure, women are more prone to blame others than men are to take responsibility for their mistakes. Men, on the other hand, prefer to take responsibility for failure based on factors beyond their control, such as the difficulty of the work at hand. More than that, women are more likely than men to look at failure in a broader sense, doubting not only one's own ability but one's overall self-worth. Women are especially averse to failure because of this.

A woman's sense of self-worth may be seriously harmed if she views each failure as a reflection of her overall aptitude or self-worth. In an effort to safeguard their sense of self-worth and self-concept, women are more inclined than males to shy away from risky endeavors.

Disrupting global and internal attributions of failures requires paying attention to thinking patterns after a failure or setback and purposefully questioning unhelpful attentions since they are habitual, careful and honest in your evaluation of what went wrong on both the external and internal levels. In addition, make sure to acknowledge the positive aspects of your performance.

Locate and Profile Positive Female Role Models

According to research, women's self-esteem and performance are positively influenced by role models. In 2013, researchers from a Swiss university challenged 149 students (81 women and 68 men) to deliver a compelling political statement against raising student fees in front of an audience of six men and six women in a virtual reality software. On the rear wall of the virtual space, some individuals found a photograph of Hillary Clinton to hang. Others saw a picture of Bill Clinton or Angela Merkel, while others saw nothing on the wall at all. Afterward, the students were asked to rate their performance based on the speech's timing and quality. Speeches were judged on fluency and body language by a different group who had no knowledge of the experiment's parameters.

Speakers and those listening to their remarks both thought that lengthier talks were more positive. When a role model was absent, males talked more slowly than women. When it came to speaking in front of Big Bill, the word could not be said. There were no more gender disparities thanks to female role models. Those shown photographs of Hillary Clinton and Angela Merkel before their talks, women made lengthier remarks and had higher self-assessment scores than when i mages of Bill Clinton or no images at all were shown. Observers from the outside also gave their remarks a better rating. Scientists have determined that women who look up to strong female role models find it easier to deal with the pressures of the workplace and stressful events like public speaking.

It was published in 2014 that Bain & Company's research on workplaces elf-confidence and ambition came to fruition. Results indicated that women had strong hopes and goals for development when they began their jobs, but this confidence quickly faded as they were near middle age Most new female workers want to be in management, but after five years, only 16% are still interested, compared to 34% of males who begin their careers with the same goal and are still interested after two or more years of experience. Male self. Confidence has decreased by a considerably lower margin throughout the same time period as female self-aspiration has plummeted.

Women's professional confidence and ambition have declined by 39percent between new and seasoned employees, compared to 23 percent for males, according to a study by Bain & Company. There is a lack of female role models in upper management, according to replies from experienced it women who took part in a survey on the topic. Having a strong female role model may help women deal with difficult circumstances in their professions.

Affirmations and Self-Talk

One of the best ways to boost your confidence and performance is to visualize yourself doing something great. The neurons in our brains, those electrically excitable cells that convey information, perceive images as if they were a real-life event, according to studies employing brain imaging. When we visualize doing something, the brain sends an impulse to our neurons, instructing them to "perform" the action in our muscles. New neural pathways are formed in the brain that allow us to do actions that are congruent with what we've seen in our minds. This helps us to achieve the desired outcome. As a consequence, all of this takes place without the need for any physical exertion.

We are energized and ready to take on this challenge. In positive psychology, positive visualization entails seeing yourself in your ideal state. It's a great way to get a handle on what you want in life. Having a clear vision of what you want to accomplish can help you determine the tangible measures you need to take to realize your ideal self.

Growth Mindset

Fear of failure may be debilitating for women; thus, it is imperative that they learn how to deal with it Mindset theory, based on the study of Carol Dweck of Stanford University, provides people with a cognitive framework for thinking about failure that is empowering rather than restrictive. According to Dweck's reserch, the key to success is not aptitude but rather whether a person feels their talents are fixed or adjustable (fixed mentality) (growth mindset). An individual's ability to perform is determined by their thinking, while an individual's ability to learn is determined by their attitude. Individuals with a fixed attitude avoid circumstances that might reveal their limits. Because of this, they're not able to push themselves to learn new things by taking chances. When you have an "everything is an opportunity to learn" perspective, you view every situation as a chance to make progress toward your objectives.

Researchers have shown that growth mindsets may be established and have a profound impact on performance. It's similar to the above-mentioned development of positive attributions of failure, which needs careful attention to one's internal dialogue and purposeful reframing of fixed mindset beliefs with more optimistic growth mindset beliefs.

Practice

Bandura's theory of self-efficacy states that mastery experiences are the primary source of self-confidence. It is the finest technique to build confidence in your ability to achieve success in a certain undertaking. If you're having trouble overcoming your fear of failure and adopting a growth mindset, try performing one scary activity every day to build up your confidence. Small victories may add up over time to help you become more resilient, so push yourself out of your comfort zone on purpose. Even little setbacks can strengthen your mental toughness. Stepping out of your comfort zone gets easier and less frightening with time.

BEAUTY & FASHION

3

Beauty and Fashion: Unveiling the Essence of Radiance

In a world where appearances hold immense sway, the concepts of beauty and fashion intertwine, captivating our senses and shaping our perceptions. Yet, true beauty transcends mere physical allure, weaving a tapestry of inner grace, self-confidence, and authentic expression.

Defining Beauty: A Multifaceted Phenomenon

Beauty is a complex and multidimensional concept that defies a single, universal definition. It is a harmonious blend of physical attributes, personal character, and inner radiance. While societal norms may dictate specific standards of beauty, true beauty lies in the eye of the beholder, a subjective experience that resonates with our sensibilities.

At its core, beauty is a reflection of one's inner self, a manifestation of confidence, kindness, and authenticity. It is the radiance that emanates from a person who embraces their unique qualities, celebrates their imperfections, and radiates a genuine warmth that touches the hearts of others.

Fashion: The Canvas of Self-Expression

Fashion, on the other hand, is the artistic expression of personal style, a canvas upon which individuals can paint their identities. It is a means of self-expression, allowing individuals to curate their outward appearance and communicate their personalities to the world.

Fashion is not merely a reflection of trends or societal norms; it is a powerful tool for self-empowerment and individuality. Through the artful selection of clothing, accessories, and grooming choices, individuals can create a visual narrative that reflects their values, aspirations, and cultural influences.

Inner Beauty: The Essence of True Radiance

While physical beauty holds undeniable allure, it is the inner beauty that truly defines an individual's character and essence. Inner beauty is a multifaceted tapestry woven from threads of kindness, empathy, resilience, and self-acceptance.

A person with inner beauty embraces their flaws and imperfections, recognizing that true beauty lies in the authenticity of their spirit. They radiate a warmth and compassion that transcends external appearances, inspiring others to embrace their unique qualities.

The Paradox of Outward Beauty and Inner Ugliness

Regrettably, there exists a paradox where individuals may possess outward beauty but harbor an inner ugliness fueled by negativity, envy, and unkindness. This dissonance between physical allure and inner turmoil can create a profound disconnect, undermining true beauty and eroding self-worth.

It is a sobering reminder that beauty is not merely skin-deep; it is a reflection of the soul. A person who harbors hatred, jealousy, or a propensity for gossiping or putting others down ultimately diminishes their radiance, casting a shadow over their true essence.

Maintaining Your Radiance: A Lifelong Journey

For many women, maintaining their radiance and attractiveness can become a challenging endeavor, m especially within the context of a committed relationship. It is a common pitfall for some individuals to neglect their self-care routines, allowing their diet, exercise regimens, and grooming habits to slip.

However, it is essential to recognize that true beauty is not solely a pursuit for attracting a partner; it is a lifelong journey of self-love and self-respect. By prioritizing self-care and nurturing both physical and emotional well-being, women can cultivate a sense of confidence and self-assurance that transcends any relationship status.

Men, as visual beings, are undoubtedly captivated by physical appearances. Still, they are also profoundly drawn to the inner radiance that shines through a woman's demeanor, her self-confidence, and her unwavering commitment to self-care.

The Power of Self-Esteem and Confidence

Beauty and fashion hold the power to influence an individual's self-esteem and overall confidence profoundly. When a person feels beautiful, both inside and out, they exude an aura of self-assurance that permeates every aspect of their lives.

This confidence not only enhances personal interactions and relationships but also empowers individuals to embrace new challenges and pursuits with fearless determination.

Conversely, low self-esteem and insecurity can cast a shadow over one's sense of beauty, perpetuating a cycle of self-doubt and diminished self-worth. Individuals must address any underlying insecurities or dissatisfactions they may have with their appearance, taking proactive steps to foster self-love and self-acceptance.

Beauty's Profound Impact on Relationships

The impact of beauty extends far beyond mere physical attraction; it has the potential to shape the dynamics and quality of personal relationships. When both partners cultivate a deep sense of self-acceptance and mutual appreciation, their relationship becomes a sanctuary of trust, respect, and emotional intimacy.

However, when one or both partners harbor insecurities or engage in behaviors that undermine the other's sense of beauty, it can create an imbalance that erodes the foundation of the relationship .Jealousy, criticism, and a lack of emotional support can sow seeds of resentment and diminish the bond between partners.

Cultivating Compassion and Empowerment

In the pursuit of true beauty, it is essential to recognize that every individual is on a unique journey, navigating their insecurities and challenges. Rather than perpetuating a culture of judgment or competition, it is imperative to cultivate an ethos of compassion, empathy, and empowerment.

By embracing the beauty within ourselves and others, we can create a ripple effect of positivity that uplifts and inspires those around us. True beauty is not a finite resource; it is an abundant well from which we can all draw strength and inspiration.

Flaws as Expressions of Authenticity

In the pursuit of perfection, it is easy to overlook the profound beauty that lies within our imperfections. Flaws and quirks are not blemishing to be concealed; instead, they are unique expressions of our individuality and authenticity.

By embracing our flaws with grace and self-acceptance, we can transform them into powerful symbols of resilience and self-love. Fashion and grooming choices can be powerful allies in this journey, allowing us to accentuate our unique features and celebrate our authentic selves.

Conclusion: Embracing the Radiance Within

Beauty and fashion are not merely superficial pursuits; they are profound expressions of self-love, self-confidence, and individuality. True beauty radiates from within, a harmonious blend of physical attributes, personal character, and inner grace.

By cultivating self-acceptance, embracing our flaws, and nurturing both our inner and outer selves, we can unlock the full potential of our radiance. It is a journey that transcends societal norms and fleeting trends, empowering us to fearlessly embrace our authentic selves and inspire others to do the same.

In the hurdles of life, beauty, and fashion interweave, creating a vibrant and empowering narrative that celebrates the diversity of human expression. Let us embrace this journey with open hearts and minds, for true beauty lies not in perfection but in the unwavering celebration of our unique and radiant selves.

DISCOVERING YOUR VALUE: A GUIDE TO REALIZING YOUR SELF-WORTH

Introduction

At a bustling international conference, a psychologist named Dr. Helen Riordan shared a compelling tale that immediately captured the room's attention. She recounted the story of a young woman, a high-flying corporate lawyer, who seemed to have it all: prestige, a lucrative salary, and social status. Yet, beneath the veneer of success, she struggled silently with feelings of inadequacy and self-doubt.

During a high-stakes meeting-one meant to be the pinnacle of her career - this woman suddenly felt overwhelmed. Despite her accomplishments, she couldn't shake the feeling that she didn't truly belong there. "I'm not good enough for this, "she thought, her self-worth teetering on the edge of a cliff.

It took one observant colleague to notice her distress and pull her aside afterward. "You are more than capable, "he insisted earnestly. "You need to see it for yourself" Inspired by this pivotal moment, she embarked on a journey to rediscover her self-worth.

This chapter delves into why understanding and embracing your self-worth is not just beneficial but essential. Like the lawyer in Dr. Riordan's story, many women navigate through life's challenges while confronting internal doubts. Here, we explore the transformative impact of self-worth on every aspect of your life-from the relationships you cherish to the dreams you pursue with vigor. This is your guide through the complex maze of self-evaluation, a journey towards finding and holding onto the profound peace that comes from truly knowing your worth.

What is Self-Worth?

Self-worth is the quiet understanding and steadfast belief in your intrinsic value as a person. It isn't determined by external markers like success, accolades, or social validation. Rather, self-worth comes from an inner conviction that you are worthy of love, respect, and care, simply because you exist. It's that gentle, unshakeable voice inside that reassures you, "You are enough, "even when external pressures and challenges suggest otherwise.

Unveiling True Instances of Self-Worth

Anecdote 1: Emily, a middle school teacher in a small town, often felt overshadowed by her college friends who had moved to bigger cities and landed high-paying jobs. Despite loving her work, she struggled with feelings of inadequacy. Everything changed when she spearheaded a community project that helped provide free meals to students during the summer break. The over whelming gratitude from the parents and the joy on her students' faces reminded her that her worth wasn't measured by income or glamour but by the profound impact she had on her community.

Anecdote 2: Lisa, a freelance graphic designer, faced constant rejection in her early career, with potential clients often opting for more established firms. The continuous cycle of no's battered her confidence. However, during a local business expo, she presented a project that addressed environmental sustainability through design, which resonated deeply with a startup looking to pioneer in green technology. Their enthusiastic feedback and subsequent partnership helped Lisa realize that her value didn't lie in universal approval but in her unique vision and commitment to causes she believed in.

Empowering Statistics

Statistics underline the significance of self-worth, especially for women navigating personal and professional spheres. For instance, research from the University of Waterloo found that women with higher self-worth are less likely to engage in harmful relationships and more likely to pursue opportunities that align with their skills and passions. Furthermore, a study by the National Association for Self-Esteem showed that women with a strong sense of self-worth are better at managing stress and overcoming adversity, highlighting how critical self-worth is to resilience and overall well-being.

A Deep Perspective on Self-Worth

Understanding self-worth is about more than recognizing your strengths - it involves embracing your whole self, Including weaknesses and past mistakes .It's about treating yourself with the same kindness and understanding you'd offer a dear friend. This perspective shifts self-worth from a concept to a practice, one that fosters a more compassionate and supportive inner dialogue.

Self-worth is also reflected in how you allow others to treat you. It means setting healthy boundaries and knowing that you deserve relationships that bring joy and growth, not diminish your spirit. Each time you assert these boundaries, you reinforce your sense of worth.

In sum, self-worth is a vital, living part of who you are. It's not just about feeling good enough; it's about knowing you deserve to take up space and pursue happiness, irrespective of the roles you play or the expectations others may have of you. This deep-seated acceptance invites a life filled with more meaningful and loving relationships, starting with the one you have with yourself.

The Interplay Between Self-Worth and Self-Love

Self-worth and self-love are inseparable concepts that fuel our inner strength and guide our interactions with the world. Self-worth is the intrinsic belief in your own value, recognizing that you deserve respect, love, and care simply because you are you. Self-love, on the other hand, is the active practices of affirming this belief through the choices you make every day choices that nurture your physical, emotional, and spiritual well-being.

Engaging in Self-Love Practices

Self-love can manifest in various meaningful actions that reflect a commitment to your personal well-being. This might include setting firm boundaries that protect your energy, pursuing passions that light up your soul, and taking care of your body and mind through healthy habits. Each act of self-love reinforces the foundational belief in your own worth.

A study underscores the profound impact of self-love on mental health. It found that women who regularly practiced self-compassion reported significantly higher levels of well-being and significantly lower levels of depression and anxiety compared to those who did not engage in self-compassionate behaviors.

The Crucial Role of Self-Worth in Relationships

Understanding and embracing your self-worth directly influences how you relate to others. When you truly recognize and appreciate your own value, you naturally gravitate towards relationships that reflect this belief. You become more likely to choose partners who respect and uplift you, and less likely to tolerate behaviors that undermine your self-esteem.

A Story of Transformation

Consider the story of Sarah, a vivid example of how self-worth can transform one's relationships. For years, Sarah found herself in a cycle of undervaluing relationships where she felt unappreciated and overlooked. The turning point came when she attended a self-worth workshop that sparked a profound realization: she had been settling because she didn't fully recognize her own worth.

Empowered by this new understanding, Sarah decided to make a change. She ended her unfulfilling relationship, a brave step that opened the door to healing and growth. With time, her newfound self-esteem led her to meet someone who truly valued her. This new relationship was marked by mutual respect and appreciation, qualities that were absent in her past interactions.

Sarah's journey is a testament to the power of recognizing one's self-worth. It not only changed the dynamics of her personal relationships but also restored her belief in herself. This transformation underscores a universal truth: understanding and practicing self-worth and self-love can dramatically improve the quality of our lives and the health of our relationships.

By embracing your intrinsic value and treating yourself with kindness and respect, you set a standard for how others should treat you. This realization is both empowering and liberating, as it fosters healthier, more fulfilling connections with those around you. The journey to self-love and self-worth is ongoing, but each step forward is a step towards a more joyful and satisfying life.

Strengthening Your Self-Worth: A Path to Inner Empowerment

Improving your self-worth is akin to embarking on a deeply personal and transformative journey. It's not something you can achieve overnight, nor is there a final destination. Rather, it's an ongoing process of introspection, healing from past wounds, and reshaping negative thought patterns into affirmations that celebrate and reinforce your intrinsic value.

The Power of Positive Affirmations

At the heart of enhancing self-worth is the practice of replacing old, self-limiting beliefs with positive affirmations. These affirmations are not just feel-good statements but powerful tools of self-transformation. They help rewrite the narrative you have about yourself, reinforcing the truth that you are valuable, capable, and deserving of respect and love.

Practical Tip: Embrace a Self-Worth Journal

One effective way to cultivate a strong sense of self-worth is by keeping a self-worth journal. This is not just any journal-it's a dedicated space for affirming your value daily.

Here's how to get started:

Choose a Journal that resonates with you. It could be beautifully designed, simple, or whatever appeals to your aesthetic sense. The key is that it should invite you to write in it.

Daily Entries: Every day, commit to writing down three things that you appreciate about yourself. These can range from personal qualities and small achievements to ways you've positively impacted others. For example:

Qualities: "I am resilient - I kept going even when things were tough today."

Achievements: "I completed a project that I've been procrastinating on for weeks."

Contributions to Others: "I listened to a friend who needed support, providing comfort."

Reflection: Regularly revisit what you've written, especially on days when you doubt your worth. This practice not only helps in recognizing your daily victories but also builds a reservoir of positive self-regard that you can draw upon during challenging times.

Emma's Journey to Self-Worth

Consider the story of Emma, who struggled with low self-esteem due to challenging relationships and past failures. Emma started a self-worth journal on the recommendation of a therapist. Initially skeptical, she soon found that jotting down her daily achievements and positive qualities became a highlight of her day. Over time, Emma noticed a shift in her mindset - she started feeling more confident and less affected by external criticism. This simple practice helped her rediscover her strengths and gradually rebuild her self-esteem.

The Impact of Self-Worth on Everyday Life

Research indicates that individuals who engage in regular self-affirmation activities exhibit higher mental resilience and better emotional health. A study from the University of Pennsylvania found that participants who wrote about their positive traits daily for a week reported increased happiness and decreased depression symptoms for up to six months later.

Strengthening your self-worth is fundamentally about recognizing and embracing your unique qualities and contributions to the world. It's a deeply rewarding endeavor that not only enhances your relationship with yourself but also enriches your interactions with others. By committing to this journey, you empower yourself to live a more fulfilled and meaningful life.

Conclusion: The Unfolding Journey to Self-Worth

Embracing your self-worth is a transformative journey that touches every corner of your existence. It is an exploration into the deepest parts of yourself, seen through a lens of compassion and respect. This journey isn't just about acknowledging your worth; it's about feeling it in your bones, understanding that you are inherently valuable and deserving of love, just as you are.

The Road to Self-Discovery

On this path, you will encounter challenges and obstacles that may shake your confidence. Yet, each step taken in recognition of your worth is a building block in constructing a resilient, empowered self. These steps are opportunities for profound growth and self-discovery, moments where you learn not just to survive but to thrive.

You Are Not Alone

It's important to remember that you are not navigating this path in isolation. Every woman walks a similar journey, marked by peaks of joy and valleys of doubt. It's in these shared experiences that we find strength. Drawing on the collective courage and support of other women can fortify your own journey, reminding you that the quest for self-worth is a shared human experience.

Take the story of Ava, a young entrepreneur who faced skepticism when she launched her own business. Despite initial failures and widespread doubt, Ava persevered, driven by a deep belief in her vision and her worth. Over time, her business flourished, becoming more than just a success story - it became a testament to her self-worth. Ava's journey illustrates that while the road may be fraught with setbacks, each challenge is a chance to reaffirm your value.

The Essence of Self-Worth

Knowing your self-worth is the cornerstone of living a life filled with passion, purpose, and peace. It is understanding that your value does not diminish because of someone else's inability to see your worth. It's about standing firm in your identity and letting this truth guide your choices and relationships.

As you continue on this journey, carry with you the knowledge that you are more than enough. You are necessary. You are a unique contribution to this world. This belief is not just a source of personal power - it's the foundation of your life's narrative.

By embracing your self-worth, you open doors to a life that is not only self-sustaining but also richly rewarding. This journey, your journey, is replete with possibilities and joys yet to be discovered. Let your realization of your own worth be the first step towards an empowered and unstoppable life.

HOW TO VALUE YOURSELF: THE ART OF SELE-VALUATION

Happiness Starts Within

The foundation of valuing oneself rests upon the fundamental realization that happiness is an internal state. It's not about acquiring external accolades or material possessions but cultivating a deep sense of contentment and fulfillment within. Start by embracing the uniqueness of your being, recognizing that your worth is inherent and independent of external validation. Understand that true happiness flourishes when you align your actions with your values and aspirations, fostering authenticity and self-compassion.

To truly value yourself, prioritize your mental, emotional, and physical wellbeing. Cultivate habits that nourish your body, mind, and soul, such as regular exercise, mindfulness practices, and healthy relationships. Invest time in activities that bring you joy and fulfillment, whether is pursuing a passion, spending time with loved ones, or simply enjoying moments of solitude.

Developing a compassionate and understanding relationship with yourself is essential for fostering inner peace and fulfillment. Treat yourself with the same kindness and empathy that you would extend to a friend in need. Embrace your imperfections as opportunities for growth and self-discovery, rather than sources of shares or inadequacy.

Valuing yourself is an ongoing journey of self-discovery, self-acceptance, and self-Hove. It requires cultivating a deep sense of happiness and wellbeing from within, prioritizing authenticity, compassion, and personal growth. By embracing your inherent worth and nurturing a loving relationship with yourself, you can unlock your full potential and live a life of fulfillment and meaning. Remember, happiness starts within – it's time to embrace the beautiful journey of self-valuation and discover the limitless possibilities that lie within you.

The Journey of Self-Discovery

To embark on the journey of self-valuation is to embark on a profound exploration of one's inner landscape. It is a journey that begins with the realization that true happiness starts within oneself. In a world often fixated on external validation and measures of success, the path to authentic self-value can seem elusive. Yet, it is within our power to uncover and nurture a deep sense of worthiness, rooted in self-compassion, understanding, and inner peace.

Embrace Self-Discovery

The first step in valuing oneself authentically is to embark on a journey of self-discovery. This entails delving into the depths of our psyche, exploring our strengths, weaknesses, passions, and fears. It requires us to embrace both the light and shadow aspects of our personality, acknowledging and integrating these facets into our sense of self. Through practices such as meditation, journaling, and introspection, we can cultivate self-awareness and unravel the layers of conditioning and societal expectations that may obscure our true essence.

Cultivate Self-Awareness

Self-awareness is the cornerstone of self-valuation. It involves developing a keen understanding of our thoughts, emotions, and behaviors without judgment or criticism. By observing ourselves with curiosity and compassion, we can gain insight into our motivations, desires, and values. This awareness empowers us to make conscious choices that align with our authentic selves, leading to a greater sense of fulfillment and purpose. The constraints of unrealistic standards and societal pressures. Instead, you can wholeheartedly celebrate your own journey, recognizing its intrinsic value and significance.

At the heart of embracing your uniqueness lies authenticity the unwavering commitment to being true to yourself in every facet of your existence. Authenticity is the beacon that guides you through life's twists and turns, illuminating the path with integrity and purpose. When you embrace your authenticity, you radiate a magnetic aura that draws others to you, fostering genuine connections and meaningful relationships.

The Power of Gratitude

Cultivating an attitude of gratitude serves as a foundational element in the construction of self-worth. It's a deliberate choice to acknowledge and appreciate the blessings and abundance that permeate our lives. By taking moments to reflect on these gifts, both big and small, we honor the richness of our existence. From the warmth of the morning sun to the laughter of loved ones, there's a myriad of simple joys and profound experiences that color our journey.

Practicing gratitude isn't merely a one-time event but a daily ritual, a conscious effort to infuse our lives with appreciation. It's about savoring the present moment, allowing ourselves to be fully immersed in the beauty of now. Whether it's a breathtaking sunset or a comforting embrace, each instance becomes an opportunity to express gratitude and deepen our connection to the world around us.

4
SELF DEVELOPMENT

SELF-DEVELOMENT AND BEING COMFORTABLE IN YOUR OWN SKIN

INTRODUCTION TO SELE-DEVELOPMENT

Self-development is the continuous journey toward becoming the best version of oneself.

It is a deliberate effort to grow, learn, and improve in various aspects of life. This journey is not just about professional success but encompasses personal growth, emotional intelligence, relationships, and overall well-being.

In a fast-paced world filled with distractions and pressures, many people struggle to find a sense of purpose and direction. The pursuit of self-development offers a path to clarity and fulfillment. It encourages us to take charge of our own destinies, fostering resilience, creativity, and adaptability. This process requires patience, self-reflection, and a commitment to growth.

UNDERSTANDING THE SELF

The foundation of self-development lies in understanding who you are. This involves examining your values, beliefs, strengths, weaknesses, and aspirations. By delving into these aspects, you can create a roadmap for your personal growth.

Take a moment to reflect on your values. What principles guide your decisions and actions?

Identifying your core values is crucial because they serve as a compass throughout your journey. As you gain clarity about your values, you begin to align your life choices with them, creating a sense of purpose and authenticity.

Another essential aspect of understanding yourself is recognizing your strengths and weaknesses. By embracing your strengths, you can leverage them to achieve your goals.

Meanwhile, acknowledging your weaknesses provides an opportunity for growth. This self-awareness is a powerful tool for self-development, allowing you to set realistic goals and wok on areas that need improvement.

SETTING GOALS FOR PERSONAL GROWTH

Setting clear, achievable goals is a critical step in the self-development journey. These goals act as milestones that guide your progress and provide a sense of direction. When setting goals, it's essential to be specific, measurable, achievable, relevant, and time-bound

(SMART).

Think about the different areas of your life where you want to grow. It could be your career, relationships, health, or personal interests. Create goals that align with your values and contribute to your overall well-being. For example, if you value health, set a goal to exercise regularly or adopt a balanced diet. If you value relationships, aim to strengthen connections with family and friends.

However, goal-setting alone is not enough. To stay motivated, you need to find your "why." What drives you to achieve these goals? Understanding your motivations adds emotional depth to your journey. It transforms your goals from mere tasks to meaningful pursuits.

When the going gets tough, remembering your "why" can reignite your passion and keep you moving forward.

BUILDING HABITS AND ROUTINES

Habits and routines play a significant role in self-development; They shape your daily life and influence your long-term success. To create positive change, you need to develop habits that align with your goals and values. This requires consistency and discipline.

Start by identifying the habits that are holding you back. It could be procrastination, negative thinking, or unhealthy behaviors. Replace these habits with positive alternatives.

For example, if you tend to procrastinate, create a daily schedule with specific time blocks for different tasks. This structure helps you stay focused and accountable.

Developing a morning routine can also set the tone for a productive day. Consider incorporating activities that promote physical and mental well-being, such as exercise, meditation, or journaling. These practices create a positive mindset and boost your energy levels.

Consistency is key when building habits. It takes time and effort to establish new routines, so be patient with yourself. Celebrate small victories along the way, as they reinforce your commitment to self-development.

EMBRACING CHANGE AND GROWTH

Self-development is a dynamic process that requires embracing change and growth. It involves stepping out of your comfort zone and taking risks. While change can be intimidating, it is often the catalyst for personal transformation.

One of the most powerful ways to embrace change is by adopting a growth mindset. This mindset believes that abilities and intelligence can be developed through effort and learning. It encourages resilience in the face of challenges and a willingness to learn from failures.

As you progress on your self-development journey, remember that setbacks are a natural part of growth. Instead of viewing failures as roadblocks, see them as opportunities to learn and improve. Embrace a mindset of curiosity and experimentation, and don't be afraid to try new things.

CULTIVATING SELF-AWARENESS

Self-awareness is the foundation of personal growth. It refers to your ability to recognize your emotions, thoughts, and behaviors, and understand how they impact you and those around you. Developing self-awareness allows you to make better decisions, build healthier relationships, and grow as a person.

METHODS FOR INCREASING SELF-AWARENESS

Mindfulness: Mindfulness involves being present in the moment and observing your thoughts and feelings without judgment. Practices such as meditation and deep breathing exercises can help you become more aware of your inner state.

Journaling: Writing down your thoughts and experiences can be a powerful tool for gaining insights into your own mind. Journaling encourages reflection and allows you to track your emotional patterns over time.

Feedback from Others: Seeking feedback from trusted friends, colleagues, or mentors can provide an external perspective on your behavior and attitudes. This feedback can reveal blind spots and help you understand how others perceive you.

Acceptance: Self- The Foundation of Confidence

Self-acceptance involves embracing your flaws, imperfections, and unique qualities. It is the foundation of confidence and a critical aspect of personal growth. When you accept yourself, you are more likely to experience a sense of inner peace and well-being.

CHALLENGES IN ACHIEVING SELF-ACCEPTANCE

Many people struggle with self-acceptance due to societal expectations and internalized negative beliefs. The pressure to conform to societal norms can lead to feelings of inadequacy. Additionally, past failures or traumatic experiences can create a sense of unworthiness. The journey to self-acceptance requires confronting these challenges and choosing to embrace who you are.

HOW SELF-ACCEPTANCE CONTRIBUTES TO WELL-BEING

Self-acceptance is closely linked to mental health and overall well-being. When you accept yourself, you are less likely to suffer from anxiety, depression, or low self-esteem. It allows you to focus on your strengths and work on areas that need improvement without harsh self-criticism. Self-acceptance also empowers you to pursue your passions and live authentically.

OVERCOMING SELF-DOUBT AND NEGATIVE BELIEFS

Self-doubt is a common barrier to personal growth and confidence. It stems from a variety of sources, including societal expectations, past failures, and constant comparison to others.

Addressing self-doubt is crucial for cultivating a positive self-image and achieving personal development.

COMMON SOURCES OF SELF-DOUBT

Societal Expectations: Society often sets unrealistic standards for success, beauty, and achievement. These expectations can lead to self-doubt when individuals feel they do not meet these standards,

Past Failures: Experiencing failure or rejection can create a fear of trying again, leading to self-doubt. The memory of past setbacks can undermine confidence and hinder progress.

Comparison to Others: Social media and other platforms often encourage comparison, which can lead to feelings of inadequacy. Constantly comparing yourself to others can diminish self-worth and fuel self-doubt.

STRATEGIES FOR OVERCOMING SELF-DOUBT

Positive Affirmations: Repeating positive affirmations can help reframe negative beliefs and build confidence. Statements like "I am capable" and "I am enough" can challenge self- doubt.

Therapy: Professional therapy provides a safe space to explore and address negative beliefs. Cognitive-behavioral therapy (CBT) and other therapeutic approaches can help reframe unhelpful thoughts.

Building a Support Network: Surrounding yourself with supportive friends, family, or mentors can boost confidence and counteract self-doubt. A strong support network offers encouragement and perspective when self-doubt arises

BE YOU: Be Unapologetically You!

Being you can be revolutionary in a world that constantly pushes us towards conformity. Being unapologetically you is not about transforming into someone else; it's about shedding the layers of societal expectations and reconnecting with your true essence.

It's about not hiding or changing to fit someone else's image of who you should be. This chapter explores the transformative journey of being unapologetically yourself, which leads to deep empowerment and self-realization.

My Journey to Being 'The Pink Lady of Oakland'

My journey to authenticity began with a bold choice: wearing pink daily. Friends, family, and even strangers confused and criticized this decision. At church, whispers of judgment echoed through the halls, suggesting my choice was bizarre or misguided. Yet, this was not just a whim but a declaration of my identity.

Despite the pressures, including a relationship that nearly demanded I abandon my pink persona for a promise of marriage, I stood firm. I cried through the hurtful comments, yet each tear also watered the seeds of my self-respect and courage. Over time, wearing pink ceased to be just a preference_ it symbolized my resilience and self-love.

This path of authenticity has led to my nickname, Pinky, and my brand, "The Pink Lady Of Oakland," which might soon inspire a show or movie. Remember, it's not about the color you wear but about embracing your unique self, no matter the shade.

The Value of Being Different

Embracing uniqueness transcends personal satisfaction and is crucial for making meaningful contributions to the world. When women stop conforming and start celebrating their traits, they unlock new opportunities for creativity and leadership, which are crucial for innovation in business and personal relationships.

1. Unleashing Creativity

Authenticity fuels creativity. For women, being true to their selves taps into a wellspring of unique ideas shaped by personal experiences. Diversity drives innovation, enhancing problem-solving and outcomes in collaborative environments. By presenting authentic selves, women can influence broader perspectives and spark new solutions in any field.

2. Leading with Authenticity

Authentic leaders are seen as more trustworthy and inspiring, creating environments where others feel safe to express and engage. This is particularly empowering where women's voices have been marginalized, transforming cultures into inclusive spaces and encouraging everyone to contribute openly.

3. Expanding Opportunities

Living authentically aligns you with opportunities that suit your unique skills and passions. This might attract collaborations and customers who value your distinct business offerings. In personal spheres, it cultivates relationships with those who genuinely support you, enhancing the quality of connections.

4. Encouraging Other Women

By choosing to be genuine, women serve as role models, inspiring others to embrace their differences. This challenges traditional norms and paves the way for a more inclusive view of success and influence, proving that our unique attributes are strengths to be celebrated.

Dealing with Judgment and Criticism

Criticism can sting, especially when it touches on our vulnerabilities. Kathy Caprino notes in her article "Let's Face it-We're Deathly Afraid of Authenticity" that our society often punishes those who stray from the norm. Yet leaders like Brene Brown remind us that many people feel alone in their struggles and crave genuine connection. You offer others the courage to do the same by being authentically you.

Here are strategies for effectively managing and responding to criticism, particularly for women who often face societal pressures and judgment.

1. Reflect and Redirect

When faced with negative comments, take a moment to reflect on the intent behind the words. Ask yourself whether the criticism is constructive or merely harmful. Use this insight to redirect your focus back to your strengths. Remember, the goal isn't to change yourself to avoid criticism but to grow and affirm your values and abilities.

2. Build Emotional Buffers

Strengthen your emotional defenses by engaging in regular self-esteem-boosting activities. This could include:

- Affirmations: Daily affirmations can reshape your internal dialogue, reinforcing a positive self-image.
- Pursuits of Passion: Invest time in activities you love that make you feel competent and accomplished. Whether it's art, sports, or any other hobby, these activities improve skills and enhance your mood and self-confidence.
- Supportive Networks: Surround yourself with people who uplift and support you. A strong support network can buffer the negative effects of external criticism.

3. Seek Constructive Feedback

Learn to distinguish between harmful criticism and constructive feedback. Constructive feedback is aimed at improvement and comes from a place of goodwill. It is specific, actionable, and relevant. Embrace such feedback as a valuable personal and professional development tool.

4. Learn and Grow

Use criticism as a learning opportunity. Analyze feedback, extract useful insights, and apply them to foster personal growth. This process improves resilience and empowers you to become more competent and self-assured.

5. Inspirational Stories

Look to stories of other women who have turned their unique traits and experiences into strengths. These narratives can provide both inspiration and practical models for handling criticism. For example, consider the stories of women leaders in various fields who have faced and overcome substantial criticism by standing firm in their personal and professional identities.

The Power of Self-Love in a Judging World

In a world often too quick to judge and slow to understand, cultivating self-love is not just beneficial; it's essential. For those committed to living authentically, self-love protects against the barrage of external opinions and criticisms.

1. Embracing Self-Acceptance

Self-acceptance is the cornerstone of self-love. It involves seeing your true self, embracing what you find, and recognizing your inherent worth independent of others' approvals or expectations. This means appreciating who you are in the present, not conditional on who you might become. When you practice self-acceptance, you affirm to yourself that you are enough, exactly as you are-an empowering and liberating message.

2. Practical Steps to Cultivate Self-Love

Mindfulness Practices: Engage in mindfulness techniques that foster an awareness of the present moment while acknowledging and accepting one's feelings, thoughts, and bodily sensations. Mindfulness can help you better understand yourself and reduce the noise of negative external judgments.

- **Self-Care Routines:** Establish routines that prioritize your well-being, such as regular exercise, adequate sleep, healthy eating, and hobbies that you love. Self-care reinforces the value you place on yourself and can significantly boost your mood and energy levels, making it easier to maintain a positive self-image.
- **Positive Social Interactions:** Surround yourself with supportive and uplifting people. Relationships that provide encouragement and understanding can enhance your sense

of self-worth and provide a refuge from the critical world outside. Choose to spend time with those who see and nurture the best in you.
- **Continuous Learning and Growth:** Invest in personal development to foster self-esteem. This could be through formal education, learning new skills, or personal exploration. Growth-focused activities build confidence and help you feel prepared to handle whatever comes your way.

3. Overcoming Negative Self-Talk

One of the biggest challenges to self-love is internalized negative self-talk--a critical inner voice that perpetuates doubt and insecurity. Combat this by:

- **Challenging Negative Thoughts:** When you think negatively about yourself, challenge these thoughts by asking for evidence of their truth. Often, you'll find these thoughts are based on misperceptions.
- **Affirmations and Positive Reinforcement:** Use positive affirmations to counteract negative thoughts. Regularly repeating phrases like "I am worthy, "I am capable," and "1 am resilient" can shift your mindset and strengthen your self-love.

4. Self-Love as Empowerment

Self-love empowers you to stand firm in your identity and make choices that reflect your true self. It transforms how you interact with the world, encouraging you to act not out of fear or desire for approval but from a place of strength and authenticity. This empowerment is especially crucial for women, who may navigate more complex social pressures and expectations.

Living Your Best Life by Being Yourself

Living authentically means aligning your daily actions with your true self and embracing your identity fully without succumbing to the expectations of others. Here's how you can live unapologetically and authentically, fostering a life that resonates with who you truly are.

1. Pursue Your Passions Fearlessly

Embrace your interests and passions wholeheartedly, regardless of how others perceive them. Whether you pursue a career that speaks to your heart, engage in a hobby that excites you, or choose a right lifestyle, what matters most is that it brings you joy and fulfillment. When you pursue what you love without seeking approval, you cultivate a sense of satisfaction and achievement that is genuinely your own.

2. Set Personal Standards and Values

Defining your standards and values is crucial to living an authentic life. Reflect on what truly matters to you, such as honesty, compassion, innovation, or resilience, and let these principles guide your decisions. By staying true to your values, you navigate life with integrity and build a life that looks good on the outside and feels right on the inside. This alignment is the essence of living authentically--it ensures that your path reflects your true self, not an image crafted to please others.

3. Create Authentic Spaces

Strive to create spaces-both personal and professional-that encourage authenticity. This could mean designing a home that reflects your personality or cultivating a workplace culture that values genuine expression and diverse voices. When spaces reflect and respect individuality, they become havens for creativity and comfort.

Nurture Relationships That Honor Your Authenticity

Foster relationships that respect and affirm your true self, which is essential for living authentically. Prioritize open communication and clear boundaries to ensure mutual respect. Surround yourself with supporters who value your uniqueness and provide emotional support. Embrace vulnerability with trusted individuals to deepen connections. These authentic relationships enhance your emotional well-being and reinforce your self-worth, supporting your journey toward a fulfilling, authentic life.

Final Thoughts:

Being unapologetically yourself is not just about personal satisfaction-it's a radical act of self-Liberation that challenges societal norms and paves the way for a fulfilling life. It's about finding peace in who you are and joy in how you express it. This chapter isn't just advice; it's a call to action to embrace your uniqueness, love yourself wholeheartedly, and live your truth daily. As you turn each page, remember: in life's journey, being yourself is not just the best choice-it's the only choice that will ever truly satisfy you.

SELF-DEVELOPMENT SECRETS: How To Cultivate A Better You!!

Self-development serves as the compass that guides us to become the best versions of ourselves in life. It's not just about career growth or academic success; it's about deepening self-awareness, honing personal strengths, and embracing our potential.

For women, this path is not merely a pursuit but a necessity in a world that often demands more from them. This chapter explores the essence of self-development, offering practical strategies to cultivate a fulfilling, empowered life.

What is Self-Development?

Self-development is the deliberate and ongoing process of enhancing one's qualities, abilities, and awareness to improve the overall quality of life. This journey involves identifying and building on your strengths while acknowledging and addressing weaknesses. It's about setting personal goals, learning new skills, and making positive changes that align with your values and aspirations.

At its core, self-development is about growth and transformation. It encompasses everything from refining practical skills and expanding knowledge to deepening emotional intelligence and fostering better relationships. This process helps individuals realize their full potential and achieve greater fulfillment and self-satisfaction.

For many women, the path of self-development is not just about personal achievement but also about enhancing self-love and strengthening relationships. t involves a continuous commitment to personal growth, which can significantly improve all areas of life, including individual and professional realms.

Different Types Of Self-Development

Self-development encompasses a variety of dimensions, each contributing uniquely to personal growth and well-being. Here's a deeper look at the different types of self-development, helping you understand how each area can enhance your life and guide your personal improvement efforts:

1. Professional Development

Professional development focuses on acquiring and refining skills to advance your career. This includes participating in training programs, attending workshops, and pursuing further education that aligns with your career goals.

Seeking challenging roles and responsibilities is also crucial, as they push you out of your comfort zone and foster skill enhancement. For women, professional development might also involve leadership training and learning to navigate and succeed in predominantly male dominated industries.

2. Emotional Development:

Emotional development is about improving emotional intelligence. It involves understanding and managing one's own emotions as well as those of others. This type of development is key for enhancing interpersonal relationships and making thoughtful decisions.

Practices such as mindfulness, therapy, and reflective journaling can aid in recognizing emotional patterns and triggers, leading to better emotional regulation and empathy.

3. Physical Development:

Physical development emphasizes maintaining and improving physical health, which significantly impacts energy levels, mental health, and overall quality of life. A fundamental aspect is regular physical activity, a nutritious diet, adequate sleep, and routine medical check-ups. For many, physical development also includes stress management, which is crucial for long-term health and vitality.

4. Intellectual Development:

Intellectual development involves engaging your mind through learning and cognitive challenges. This can be achieved by exploring new subjects, reading extensively, and pursuing hobbies that require mental engagement, such as puzzles, games, or learning a new language.

Keeping the mind active enhances knowledge and stimulates cognitive functions, helping prevent mental decline as you age.

5. Social Development:

Social development focuses on improving your ability to form and maintain healthy relationships.

It involves developing skills like communication, active listening, and conflict resolution. Engaging in community service, participating in group activities, and nurturing supportive friendships are all part of social development. This can also mean building networks supporting professional growth and personal enrichment for women.

6. Spiritual Development:

Though not applicable to everyone, spiritual development can play a significant role in self- development for those who seek it. This might involve exploring one's beliefs, values, and sense of purpose through meditation, religious practice, or spiritual gatherings. Spiritual development, purpose through meditation, religious practice, or spiritual gatherings. Spiritual development helps many find a deeper sense of peace and understanding, fostering holistic well-being.

Strategies To Improve Their Self-Development

Self-development is a dynamic process that requires commitment, insight, and a structured approach to truly flourish. Here are comprehensive strategies to guide you on this path, helping ensure that your growth journey is as rewarding as it is transformative.

1. Assess Your Strengths and Weaknesses

Self-awareness is the bedrock of self-development. Start by conducting a detailed and honest evaluation of your strengths and areas for improvement. Use tools like reflective journaling. feedback from trusted friends or colleagues, and personality assessments to better understand yourself.

Recognize patterns in your behavior, and pay attention to when you feel most vulnerable and competent. For example, if public speaking is challenging, acknowledging this fear is the first step toward targeted improvement, such as joining a speaking club or taking communication classes.

2. Set Personal Goals

Goal setting is critical in steering your self-development efforts. Ensure your goals are SMART: Specific, Measurable, Achievable, Relevant, and Time-bound. Align these objectives with your values and long-term aspirations.

Consider setting goals across different life areas such as career, health, education, and personal relationships to maintain balanced growth. For instance, if you aim to improve your health, set a specific goal to exercise thrice a week for 30 minutes.

3. Create a Development Plan

With your goals specified, draft a comprehensive plan that outlines the steps, resources, and timelines needed to achieve them. Your plan should be flexible to accommodate new insights and charging circumstances. Regularly review and adjust your plan to ensure it stays aligned with your personal and professional objectives. Include short-term tasks and long-term milestones to keep track of progress and maintain motivation.

4. Embrace Lifelong Learning

Commit to lifelong learning by engaging in various educational and developmental activities. This could involve formal education, such as courses and certifications, and informal learning, like reading, attending workshops, or online tutorials. Experiment with new hobbies that challenge your creativity and intellectual capacities, such as learning a musical instrument or a new language, which can enhance cognitive flexibility and problem-solving skills.

5. Seek Feedback and Mentorship

Feedback is essential for growth. Regularly seek constructive criticism from mentors, peers, and even juniors, which can provide diverse perspectives on your performance and development. Establish mentor relationships with individuals who have the expertise and empathy to foster your growth. Effective mentorship can guide, motivate, and support you as you navigate your personal and professional challenges.

6. Prioritize Health and Wellness

Your physical and mental healths are crucial to sustaining effective self-development. Integrate regular physical activity, balanced nutrition, and sufficient rest into your routine. Address mental health by practicing mindfulness, stress reduction techniques, and maintaining social connections. Activities like yoga, meditation, and time in nature can rejuvenate the mind and body, enhancing overall well-being.

7. Cultivate a Growth Mindset

Develop a growth mindset by embracing challenges and viewing failures as opportunities for learning. Understand that abilities and intelligence can be developed through dedication and persistence. This mindset encourages resilience, facilitates positive feedback responses, and fosters a commitment to continuous improvement.

8. Network and Build Relationships

Networking is vital for both personal and professional development. It extends beyond merely advancing your career. It's about exchanging ideas, learning from others' experiences, and building supportive relationships. Actively participate in industry conferences, join professional groups, and participate in community activities. These connections can offer new opportunities and insights that propel your growth.

9. Manage Time Effectively

Effective time management is critical to achieving your development goals. Prioritize tasks based on their relevance to your goals and their impact. Utilize organizational tools like digital planners, apps, or the Pomodoro Technique to enhance focus and productivity. Saying no to non-essential tasks frees up resources for more critical activities.

10. Reflect and Adapt

Make regular reflection a crucial part of your routine. Set aside time to contemplate what you've learned and how you've progressed toward your goals. Assess what strategies have worked and what haven't, and be prepared to adjust your plans accordingly. This ongoing process of reflection and adaptation is crucial for staying relevant and responsive to your evolving needs and circumstances.

Cultivating Self-Love Through Self-Development

Self-love is not just a beneficial byproduct of self-development; it's a foundational aspect that fuels and sustains your growth journey. Here's how you can cultivate self-love effectively:

- **Recognize and Celebrate Progress:** Regularly acknowledge your achievements, regardless of size. Celebrating these wins boosts morale and motivation, reinforcing the importance of your efforts.
- **Develop Self-Compassion:** Treat yourself with the kindness you would offer a friend. Replace self-criticism with compassion, especially during setbacks, to enhance resilience and encourage a positive self-view.
- **Set Boundaries for Self-Care:** Learn to say "no" to protect your time and energy. Setting healthy boundaries is a critical form of self-respect and is essential for maintaining your well-being.
- **Engage in Self-Awareness Practices**: Increase self-awareness through journaling, meditation, or therapy. Understanding your emotional and mental states is key to making informed decisions that reflect your needs.
- **Prioritize Physical and Mental Health:** Good physical and mental healths are foundational for self-love. Prioritize your well-being by maintaining a healthy diet, regular exercise, and sufficient rest, and seek professional help if needed.

- **Embrace Your Uniqueness:** Acknowledge and celebrate what makes you unique. Appreciating your traits boosts self-esteem and contributes to a deeper sense of self-love.
- **Continue to Learn and Grow:** View life as a continuous learning journey. Embracing new experiences and seeking personal growth shows a commitment to improving yourself and living fully.

Over To You:

For women seeking to empower themselves, the secrets to self-development lie in consistent, mindful efforts to grow. It's about creating a personalized blueprint that respects your unique journey and aspirations.

By committing to this path, you will enhance your own life and inspire those around you. Embrace the journey of self-development as a lifelong commitment to becoming the best version of yourself- a quest that is as rewarding as it is transformative.

A Guide To Self-Esteem And Increasing Your Confidence!!

In today's fast-paced world, self-esteem and confidence are more than just buzzwords; they are foundational elements that can shape one's life trajectory. For women, cultivating these qualities is essential, not only for personal satisfaction but also for navigating the challenges of daily life.

This chapter delves deep into understanding and enhancing self-esteem and confidence, providing actionable strategies for embracing a more empowered self.

What is Self-Esteem?

Self-esteem is a deeply rooted self-perception that significantly impacts how you view your worth and capabilities. It is the sum of your self-respect, self-worth, and personal value, reflecting how much you appreciate and like yourself regardless of external circumstances. High self-esteem involves a positive yet realistic evaluation of oneself, acknowledging strengths and accepting weaknesses without undue criticism.

Significance of High Self-Esteem

High self-esteem is vital for psychological well-being and a fulfilling life. It is foundational in shaping not only one's choices but also the quality of one's relationships and overall mental health.

High self-esteem makes you more likely to set and achieve ambitious goals because you believe in your ability to succeed. It enhances your resilience, enabling you to bounce back from setbacks and failures with a perspective that is less about self-blame and more about growth and learning.

Key Practices For Developing High Self-Esteem

Building self-esteem is crucial for personal development and achieving a fulfilling life. It empowers you to embrace your worth and live authentically. Here, we delve deeper into practical strategies to strengthen your self-esteem, ensuring each step contributes to a more confident and positive self-image.

1. Positive Self-Talk

Your inner dialogue has a profound impact on your self-esteem. Negative self-talk can erode self-confidence, while positive affirmations reinforce your value. Begin by observing the tone and content of your thoughts.

When you engage in negative self-talk, actively challenge these thoughts and replace them with affirmations that celebrate your strengths and accomplishments. Phrases like "I am capable" and "I am worthy of good things" can shift your mindset towards a more positive self-view.

2. Achievement Journaling

Keeping a journal of your achievements and positive feedback is a tangible way to enhance your sense of worth. Regularly jotting down even small successes helps to solidify your abilities and achievements in your mind. This practice boosts your current self-esteem and serves as a motivational tool when facing future challenges.

3. Self-Compassion

Practicing self-compassion involves treating yourself with the same kindness and understanding you would offer a close friend. Acknowledge that setbacks and mistakes are part of the human experience and allow yourself space to learn and grow without harsh self-judgment. Techniques such as mindfulness meditation can help you develop a more compassionate approach to dealing with personal failures.

4. Set Realistic Goals

Establishing and achieving realistic goals fosters a sense of accomplishment and satisfaction. Start by setting small, manageable goals that you can build upon. This approach enhances your belief in your capabilities and keeps you motivated and engaged in your development journey. Celebrate each achievement, no matter how small, to reinforce your progress.

5. Regular Physical Activity

Engaging in regular physical activity can significantly boost self-esteem. Exercise releases endorphins, chemicals in your brain that revitalize your spirit and make you feel good. Additionally, the physical benefits of exercise, such as improved strength and stamina, can enhance your body image and self-confidence.

6. Seek Constructive Feedback

Instead of shying away from feedback, seek it proactively. Constructive criticism can be a valuable tool for personal growth. Engage with peers, mentors, or coaches who can provide honest and helpful feedback. Use this input to refine your skills and strategies, reinforcing your commitment to personal improvement.

7. Expand Your Skills

Whether through formal education or self-taught pursuits, investing in skill development can significantly enhance your self-esteem. Learning new skils makes you more competent and versatile, opening up new opportunities for growth and achievement.

8. Build Supportive Relationships

Surround yourself with people who uplift and support you. Positive relationships can reinforce your self-worth and encourage you during difficult times. Cultivate friendships and professional relationships with individuals who appreciate and respect your value.

What is Confidence?

Confidence is more than just a feeling; it's a fundamental belief in your abilities and judgment. It encompasses a sense of self-assurance that arises not from outward appearance but from an internal acknowledgment of your capabilities. This intrinsic belief enables you to face challenges, engage in new experiences, and assert your presence in various aspects of life.

Confidence allows you to trust your decision-making processes, navigate complexities clearly, and effectively communicate your thoughts and ideas. It is not a static trait but a dynamic state that can grow and diminish with life's experiences

The Importance of Confidence:

At its core, confidence is a driving force behind personal and professional growth. It fuels your willingness to take risks and step out of your comfort zone, essential for personal growth and career advancement. Confident individuals are more likely to pursue promotions, engage in challenging projects, and advocate for themselves and their ideas.

In relationships, confidence enables you to set and maintain healthy boundaries, communicate your needs effectively, and make decisions that reflect your values and desires. It contributes to a healthier self-image and promotes resilience against the pressures and criticisms of everyday life.

Moreover, confidence is contagious; it improves your life and inspires those around you. It enhances leadership qualities, making you a role model for others who may seek to emulate your self-assurance and positivity.

How To Increase Confidence?

As you have explored the journey toward personal growth, understanding the roots of self-esteem naturally leads us to the next crucial step: enhancing our confidence. Let's dive into practical strategies that can empower you to navigate life's challenges with greater assurance and boldness.

Here's how to actively increase your confidence and transform your approach to personal and professional arenas.

1. Prepare and Practice:
Preparation and practice are fundamental to developing confidence. Whether you're preparing for a public speaking event, a job interview, or any professional task, thorough preparation helps mitigate anxiety and builds self-assurance.

This includes researching your topics extensively, rehearsing your presentation or responses, and seeking opportunities for simulated practice. Feedback from these sessions can be invaluable, allowing you to refine your approach and improve your delivery, boosting your confidence.

2. Visualize Success:
Visualization is not just about imagining success; it's about engaging all your senses to create a detailed and realistic experience of achieving your goals. Practice this technique regularly by setting

aside quiet time to close your eyes and vividly imagine yourself succeeding in specific scenarios.

Focus on the details-the environment, the sounds, your emotions, and the reactions of others to enhance the realism of the experience. This practice helps condition your mind to maintain a positive outlook and a success-oriented mentality.

3. Assertiveness Training:

Assertiveness is key to effective communication and confidence. It involves expressing your thoughts and needs clearly and respectfully, without passivity or aggression. To develop this skill, start by recognizing your rights and respecting others' rights.

Engage in role-playing exercises to practice your responses to different situations, and consider taking formal training or workshops to enhance your assertiveness. This skill boosts your confidence in personal interactions and improves your relationships and workplace dynamics.

4. Celebrate Small Victories:

Recognizing and celebrating small victories is crucial for building long-term confidence. Make it a habit to acknowledge even the most minor successes each day, whether completing a task you've been postponing or handling a complex interaction well. This builds a culture of recognition for your efforts and progress, reinforcing your self-esteem and confidence over time.

5. Mentorship and Role Models:

Identify and engage with mentors and role models who exhibit the confidence you aim to achieve. These individuals can provide inspiration, practical advice, and support based on their experiences. Regular interactions with mentors can offer insights that reshape your perspective and encourage risk-taking, enhancing self-confidence.

6. Continuous Learning and Improvement:
Confidence grows with competence. Dedicate yourself to lifelong learning by taking courses, attending workshops, and reading extensively. Each new skill and piece of knowledge you acquire builds your competence and, consequently, your confidence. Additionally, embrace feedback as a tool for continuous improvement, allowing you to refine your skills and approaches effectively.

7. Adaptability to Change:
In a rapidly changing world, adaptability is a critical component of confidence. Develop flexibility by putting yourself in new and challenging situations that require adapting and learning. Reflect on past experiences where you successfully navigated change, and use these as evidence of your capability to handle future uncertainties. This resilience bolsters your confidence and prepares you to face life's unpredictability with a proactive mindset.

Synergizing Self-Worth and Capability

Self-esteem and confidence are interconnected and essential for personal development. Self-esteem is your internal sense of worth, influencing how you value and respect yourself. Confidence relates to your belief in achieving goals, affecting how you handle challenges.

For women, the relationship between self-esteem and confidence is incredibly transformative, impacting everything from personal relationships to professional advancement. High self-esteem supports confidence, encouraging assertive behavior and effective communication, while confidence reinforces self-esteem through successes and overcoming challenges.

Cultivating both involves positive self-talk, self-compassion, skill mastery, and stepping out of comfort zones. This synergy fosters personal fulfillment and empowers broader contributions in professional and community settings.

Final Thought

Now that you have the tools and understanding to enhance your self-esteem and confidence, It's over to you. Remember, the journey to self-improvement is continuous and deeply personal. Each steps build stronger foundation for a more confident, empowered, and fulfilled life.

Embrace the journey with enthusiasm and patience, knowing each email victory contributes your grand vision of who you can become.

Embracing Self-Compassion and Self-Care

Embracing self-compassion and self-care is not just an act of indulgence; it's a vital necessity for women navigating the complexities of pain and distress. In a world that often glorifies busyness and self-sacrifice, women are frequently conditioned to prioritize the needs of others at the expense of their own well-being. However, this pattern of neglecting oneself can have detrimental effects on both physical and mental health. Therefore, it's essential for women to recognize that self-care is not selfish but rather a fundamental act of self-preservation and self-respect.

Setting boundaries is a crucial aspect of self-care, allowing women to protect their time, energy, and emotional well-being from external demands and pressures. This may involve learning to say no to commitments that exceed our capacity, delegating tasks to others, or simply taking time for solitude and introspection when needed. By establishing clear boundaries, women create space for rest, replenishment, and rejuvenation, enabling them to show up more fully in their relationships, work, and personal endeavors.

Self-compassion serves as a guiding principle in the practice of self-care, offering a gentle and nurturing approach to ourselves in moments of struggle and suffering. Instead of berating ourselves for perceived shortcomings or failures, self-compassion invites us to extend kindness, understanding, and acceptance towards ourselves, just as we would to a beloved friend or family member in need. Through the cultivation of self-compassion, women build a foundation of resilience and inner strength from which to navigate life's challenges with grace and dignity, knowing that they are worthy of love and care simply by virtue of their humanity.

Seeking Support and Connection

No woman should have to bear her pain alone. Seeking support and connection is an essential aspect of navigating pain and healing for women. The journey through adversity can feel isolating and overwhelming, but reaching out to others for support can provide a vital lifeline of empathy, validation, and companionship. Whether it's confiding in a trusted friend, seeking guidance from a family member, or joining a support group of individuals who share similar experiences, connecting with others who understand and empathize with our struggles can offer a profound sense of solace and solidarity.

Sharing our stories, our struggles, and our triumphs with others not only helps to alleviate feelings of loneliness and isolation but also fosters a sense of belonging and connection. Through open and honest communication, we create a safe space for vulnerability and authenticity, where we can express our emotions without fear of judgment or rejection. In the process, we discover that we are not alone in our pain, and that there is strength and resilience to be found in the collective experience of shared suffering and healing.

Moreover, seeking support and connection allows women to tap into a vast network of resources, wisdom, and guidance that can facilitate their journey towards healing and wholeness. Whether it's practical advice on coping strategies, recommendations for therapeutic modalities, or simply a listening ear and a shoulder to lean on, the support of others can provide invaluable insights and perspectives that we may not have considered on our own.

Conclusion

In conclusion, the journey of turning pain into power is one that demands courage, resilience, and a willingness to confront the depths of our emotions and experiences. It's a path marked by uncertainty and challenge, yet within its crucible lies the transformative potential to emerge stronger, wiser, and more compassionate than before.

Through the process of acknowledging our pain, embracing vulnerability, and seeking support and connection, women can harness the power of their suffering to catalyze personal growth and inner strength. By reframing adversity as an opportunity for renewal and reinvention, women reclaim agency over their lives and chart a new course towards happiness and fulfillment.

May this guide serve as a beacon of hope and inspiration to all women who have known the depths of pain? May it remind them that within their darkest moments lies the promise of a brighter tomorrow—a tomorrow shaped not by the trials of the past, but by the resilience, courage, and compassion that they embody? As women continue on their journey of healing and wholeness, may they find solace in the knowledge that they are not alone, and that their pain has the power to ignite a flame of transformation that illuminates the path ahead.

5

TRANSFORMING PAIN INTO POWER
A guide to overcoming
Adversity and finding strength

Introduction:

In the journey of life, pain is an inevitable companion. Women often bear the weight of numerous challenges and heartaches. From the pain of broken relationships to the grief of losing loved ones, women navigate a myriad of emotions that can leave them feeling shattered and defeated. Yet, within this pain lies an extraordinary source of power—a power to transform adversity into opportunity, to rise above circumstances, and to emerge stronger than ever before. In this guide, we will explore how women can harness their pain for personal growth and resilience, offering hope and inspiration to those who are struggling to heal.

Acknowledging the Power of Pain

In acknowledging the power of pain, it's crucial to recognize the unique societal pressures and expectations that women often face. From a young age, girls are socialized to be caretakers, nurturers, and pillars of strength for their families and communities. They are taught to prioritize the needs of others above their own, to suppress their emotions, and to maintain a façade of composure even in the face of adversity.

This societal conditioning can create a paradoxical relationship with pain for many women. On one hand, they are expected to be resilient, self-sacrificing, and endlessly capable of shouldering burdens without complaint. On the other hand, they are discouraged from openly expressing vulnerability, sadness, or anger, lest they be perceived as weak or inadequate. As a result, women may internalize their pain, burying it beneath layers of stoicism and denial in an attempt to conform to societal expectations.

However, denying or minimizing our pain only serves to compound our suffering. Emotions that are suppressed or ignored do not simply disappear; instead, they fester beneath the surface, exerting a corrosive influence on our mental, emotional, and physical well-being. By acknowledging the power of our pain and allowing ourselves to feel and express our emotions authentically, we reclaim agency over our own experiences and create space for healing and growth.

This process of acknowledgment begins with self-awareness and self-compassion. It requires women to recognize that their pain is valid and deserving of acknowledgment, regardless of whether it conforms to societal norms or expectations.

Moreover, acknowledging the power of pain also involves challenging the limiting beliefs and narratives that society imposes upon women. It means rejecting the notion that vulnerability is synonymous with weakness and embracing the truth that vulnerability is, in fact, a source of strength and resilience. It means dismantling the myth of the "strong woman" who stoically bears her burdens in silence and instead celebrating the courage and authenticity of those who dare to show their wounds and ask for help.

Navigating the Pain of Divorce

Navigating the pain of divorce is a journey fraught with emotional upheaval and uncertainty. For many women, divorce represents not only the end of a marriage but also the loss of a shared future, dreams, and identity. It can leave them feeling adrift, vulnerable, and overwhelmed by a myriad of conflicting emotions.

However, within the depths of this pain lies the potential for profound transformation and growth. By reframing divorce as an opportunity for renewal and reinvention, women can harness their inner strength and resilience to navigate this challenging transition and emerge stronger, wiser, and more empowered than before.

One of the first steps in navigating the pain of divorce is to seek support from trusted friends, family members, or professional counselors. Sharing our experiences and emotions with others can provide invaluable validation, perspective, and guidance as we navigate the complexities of divorce. It can also help to alleviate feelings of isolation and loneliness, reminding us that we are not alone in our struggles and that there is hope for the future.

Additionally, exploring new interests and passions can be a powerful way to rediscover our sense of self and purpose in the aftermath of divorce. Whether it's taking up a new hobby, pursuing further education, or embarking on a journey of self-discovery through travel or creative expression, embracing new experiences can help to fill the void left by the end of a marriage and provide a sense of fulfillment and joy. Perhaps most importantly, navigating the pain of divorce requires a commitment to self-love and acceptance.

Ultimately, navigating the pain of divorce is not about pretending that the pain doesn't exist or rushing to "get over it." It's about honoring our emotions, embracing the challenges of the journey, and trusting in our own resilience and capacity for growth.

Coping with the Loss of a Child or Mother

Coping with the loss of a child or mother is an unimaginable ordeal that can shake the very foundation of one's being. The bond between a mother and her child is one of the most profound and enduring relationships in human experience, and the void left by its absence can feel insurmountable. Similarly, the loss of a mother, who often serves as a source of unconditional love, guidance, and support, can leave a gaping hole in the lives of her loved ones.

In the wake of such profound loss, it's natural for women to experience a range of overwhelming emotions, including grief, anger, guilt, and despair. These emotions may ebb and flow in unpredictable waves, leaving women feeling adrift in a sea of sorrow and confusion. Yet, it is precisely in these darkest moments that the seeds of resilience and strength are sown.

One of the most important aspects of coping with the loss of a child or mother is to honor their memory and legacy. This may involve creating rituals or traditions to commemorate their life, such as planting a tree in their honor, dedicating a memorial bench or plaque, or holding an annual remembrance ceremony with family and friends. By keeping their memory alive in our hearts and minds, we ensure that they are never truly gone and that their spirit continues to guide and inspire us in our daily lives.

Finding solace in community and support groups can also be a lifeline for women navigating the pain of loss. Connecting with others who have experienced similar losses can provide a sense of understanding, validation, and companionship that is often difficult to find elsewhere. These support networks offer a safe space for women to share their stories, express their emotions, and seek comfort and guidance from those who have walked a similar path.

6 FEMINITY

WHAT IS FEMINITY

Femininity encompasses a complex array of characteristics, behaviors, and roles traditionally associated with women and girls. It is a culturally constructed concept that has evolved overtime, reflecting societal norms, expectations, and values. At its core, femininity represents a set of traits that are often linked to softness, nurturing, empathy, and gentleness, but it can also include qualities like strength, resilience, and determination.

Historically, femininity has been tied to traditional gender roles, where women were expected to focus on domestic responsibilities, care giving, and maintaining social harmony. However, contemporary understandings of femininity are more expansive and inclusive, recognizing that gender expression varies widely among individuals.

In today's context, femininity is seen as a fluid and dynamic concept allowing women to define their own identities and break free from rigid stereotypes. Women can embody both traditionally feminine traits and characteristics typically associated with masculinity, emphasizing the spectrum of gender expression.

The recognition of diverse forms of femininity has led to a broader acceptance of gender diversity and non-binary identities. It underscores the importance of respecting individual choices and recognizing that femininity, like masculinity, is not a fixed or universal standard, but rather a unique and personal expression of self.

WHY IS FEMINITY IMPORTANT

Femininity plays a significant role in shaping individual identity and societal dynamics. It encompasses a broad range of traits, behaviors, and roles traditionally associated with women and girls. However, it is essential to recognize that femininity is not a monolithic concept, and its expression can vary widely across different cultures, periods, and individual experiences.

The importance of femininity lies in its capacity to foster a sense of belonging and connection among those who identify with it. It can serve as a source of empowerment, allowing individuals to embrace qualities such as empathy, compassion, nurturing, and creativity. These attributes are often valued in personal and professional relationships, contributing to a more cohesive and harmonious social fabric.

Additionally, femininity can challenge traditional gender norms and stereotypes, providing a platform for diverse forms of expression. As societies continue to evolve, the redefinition and expansion of femininity can lead to greater gender equity and inclusivity, promoting a more balanced and just world.

Ultimately, the significance of femininity extends beyond individual identity. It influences broader cultural narratives, inspiring shifts in perspectives and encouraging acceptance of a wider spectrum of gender identities and expressions. By embracing and valuing femininity, societies can move toward greater inclusivity and understanding.

EXAMPLES OF FEMINITY

Femininity encompasses a set of attributes, behaviors, and roles generally associated with women and girls. These characteristics can vary across cultures and periods but often include qualities traditionally linked to women's roles and identity.

Below are some examples of femininity:

Appearance and Fashion: Femininity is often expressed through clothing, hairstyles, and makeup that emphasize grace, softness, and delicacy. Dresses, skirts, and blouses in soft colors or with floral patterns are traditionally considered feminine attire.

Behavior and Mannerisms: Femininity can be reflected in behavior such as gentleness, empathy, and nurturing tendencies. This can manifest in softer speech, attentiveness to others' needs, and a caring attitude towards family and friends.

Roles and Responsibilities: Historically, femininity has been linked with roles such as care giving, parenting, and homemaking. Although these associations are evolving, many cultures still regard nurturing and supporting others as feminine traits.

Interests and Activities: Femininity is often associated with certain hobbies and interests like cooking, fashion, crafts, and social activities. Women who engage in these pursuits may be considered more feminine in certain cultural contexts.

Social Expectations: Society often reinforces certain expectations of femininity, encouraging women to be polite, compassionate, and supportive. These expectations influence how women are perceived and how they navigate personal and professional environments.

Overall, femininity is a complex and dynamic concept that varies with culture, personal identity, and changing societal norms.

ASPECTS OF FEMINITY

Femininity encompasses a broad spectrum of characteristics, behaviors, and cultural norms associated with being female or feminine. While definitions can vary across cultures and individual beliefs, common aspects of femininity often include:

Empathy and Compassion: Femininity often emphasizes the ability to understand and share the feelings of others, fostering empathy and compassion in relationships and communities.

Emotional Intelligence: This includes the capacity to recognize, understand, and manage emotions, both personal and those of others, contributing to healthier relationships.

Strength and Resilience: Femininity encompasses the inner strength and resilience to overcome challenges, adapt, and persist in the face of adversity.

Creativity and Expression: Femininity encourages creative expression through music, writing, and other forms of self-expression, allowing for unique and imaginative perspectives.

Nurturing and Care giving: This involves a natural inclination towards nurturing and caring for others, whether in a family setting, in friendships, or in professional care giving roles.

Collaboration and Cooperation: Femininity often emphasizes teamwork, cooperation, and the ability to work harmoniously with others to achieve common goals.

Intuition and Insight: Femininity is associated with intuition, offering valuable insights and a deeper understanding of situations and people.

Elegance and Grace: This includes poise, refinement, and a sense of beauty in actions, speech, and demeanor.

Community and Connection: Femininity encourages building strong social connections, fostering a sense of community, and creating supportive networks.

Diversity and Inclusivity: Femininity embraces diversity, celebrating different cultures, identities, and perspectives, contributing to a more inclusive society.

It's important to recognize that femininity is not limited to a single definition. It encompasses a range of identities and expressions, allowing for flexibility and individuality. Additionally, femininity can be displayed by people of al genders, challenging traditional gender stereotypes.

While these aspects describe traditional views of femininity, it's essential to acknowledge that femininity is not a rigi or universal concept. Women and men can express feminine traits, and individuals have the freedom to define what femininity means to them.

HOW DOES FEMINITY AFFECT OUR LOVE LIFE, MARRIAGE AND RELATIONSHIP

Femininity, a complex and multi-faceted concept, can significantly impact love life, marriage, and relationships in various ways. The effects depend on cultural, societal, and individual beliefs about gender roles and expectations. Here's an overview of how femininity might affect these aspects of life:

LOVE LIFE

- **Expression of Emotion:** Femininity typically emphasizes a stronger focus on emotional expression. This emphasis can create an environment where individuals feel more comfortable sharing their feelings, which can result in more open communication and a deeper emotional connection within relationships. People who exhibit feminine traits are often seen as more in touch with their emotions, contributing to a supportive atmosphere.
- **Communication Styles**: Traits commonly associated with femininity, such as empathy, listening, and nurturing, contribute to enhanced communication within relationships. This empathetic approach encourages understanding and allows partners to connect on a more intimate level. By fostering these feminine qualities, communication becomes more effective and meaningful, leading to greater emotional intimacy.
- **Dating Dynamics**: In various cultures, femininity aligns with specific societal expectations impacting the dynamics of dating and relationship. These expectations might influence who initiates romantic gestures or plans dates, which can, in turn, affect the flow and balance of a relationship. As a result, traditional feminine traits may play a role in shaping romantic interactions and setting the tone for courtship and relationship building.

MARRIAGE

- **Roles and Responsibilities:** Traditional views of femininity often portray women as primary caregivers and homemakers, responsible for cooking, cleaning, and raising children. These expectations can lead to a conventional division of labor within a marriage, where men are seen as breadwinners. This rigid delineation can impact relationship satisfaction, sometimes causing stress or resentment if partners have differing views on gender roles.
- **Emotional Support:** Feminine traits often encompass the ability to provide nurturing and emotional support, essential for fostering a harmonious marriage. These traits can include empathy, compassion, and attentive listening, allowing for a deeper connection between partners. When these qualities are present in a marriage, they contribute to emotional balance and strengthen the bond between spouses.
- **Decision-Making:** In relationships characterized by traditional gender roles, the concept of femininity can play a significant role in determining who holds authority and how decisions aremade.This dynamic often shapes the power balance within a marriage, with traditional expectations possibly leading to a tendency for men to make key decisions while women may have a more supportive or nurturing role.

RELATIONSHIPS

Nurturing and Care: Femininity encompasses a range of qualities, such as empathy, compassion, and intuition, which contribute to a nurturing atmosphere in relationships. This nurturing aspect fosters emotional intimacy; enabling partners to feel valued and understood. The supportive environment created through femininity promotes personal growth, encouraging mutual care and the flourishing of deeper connections.

- **Interdependence**: Femininity is often associated with qualities that encourage interdependence and collaboration, leading to a

stronger emphasis on partnership and teamwork within relationships. These traits can foster a nurturing environment where empathy and emotional support are valued, promoting open communication and a sense of unity among individuals working or living together.
- **Social Expectations:** Cultural expectations regarding femininity often dictate distinct roles and behaviors for men and women, shaping the dynamics of relationships. Women might be expected to embody traits such as nurturing and emotional sensitivity, while men might face pressures to be strong and stoic. These societal norms can create imbalances in relationships, affecting communication, division of responsibilities, and even career choices. The resulting pressures can lead to tension and misunderstandings, as couples navigate these prescribed roles and negotiate their own unique paths within the broader cultural context.

POTENTIAL CHALLENGES

- **Gender Stereotypes:** Rigid gender stereotypes associated with femininity impose predefined roles and expectations, often confining women to specific behaviors and limiting their potential. These stereotypes can perpetuate unequal power dynamics in relationships, marginalize women in professional settings, and stifle their unique expressions. This results in a society that restricts diversity and upholds systemic biases, impeding true equality.
- **Imbalance in Roles:** When traditional gender roles are rigidly enforced, it can lead to an unequal distribution of responsibilities, where one partner might bear a disproportionate share of domestic or decision-making duties. This imbalance can create tension and undermine relationship satisfaction, as it may leave one partner feeling overburdened or undervalued, impacting overall harmony.

- **Expectations and Autonomy:** When society places a strong emphasis on traditional notions of femininity, it can create a set of expectations that restricts personal autonomy and choice. This, in turn, might lead to feelings of constraint and dissatisfaction, limiting the paths available to women and ultimately impacting their overall happiness and sense of fulfillment.
- Femininity encompasses a range of traits and behaviors traditionally associated with women, such as nurturing, empathy, and compassion. In relationships, these qualities can positively influence love life, marriage, and partnerships by fostering emotional intimacy, support, and understanding.

When individuals embrace femininity in a balanced manner, it can lead to harmonious interactions where both partners feel valued and heard. However, if femininity is overly stereotyped or imposed, it can contribute to imbalanced dynamics, where gender roles restrict personal expression or limit opportunities for growth. Thus, the impact of femininity on relationships depends on embracing authenticity, respecting individuality, and acknowledging cultural and personal beliefs.

The Magic Of Feminine Energy!!

In the realm of professional communications, it's a common suggestion to women: avoid exclamation marks to be taken more seriously. This advice embodies a broader societal expectation that femininity must be downplayed for women to be regarded as competent.

However, this guidance not only undermines authentic expression but also reinforces the damaging myth that femininity is an obstacle to professional progress. This chapter delves into the sacred balance of feminine and masculine energies, exploring how embracing our complete energetic spectrum can lead to a richer, more balanced life.

The Cultural Dichotomy of Energy

Historically, the traits associated with masculinity such as assertiveness, competitiveness, and stoicism—have been valorized, often at the expense of feminine qualities like empathy, nurturing, and intuition. This bias manifests in various societal norms and practices that undervalue feminine energy.

Rachel Rossitto, a holistic healer, highlights how this imbalance can leave individuals feeling depleted not only physically but also emotionally and spiritually. The demand to monitor and adjust one's femininity can be exhausting and is a challenge that many face without even realizing its profound impact on their holistic well-being.

The Sacredness of Feminine Energy

Feminine energy, often misunderstood and undervalued in our fast-paced, results-driven society, encompasses qualities that are crucial for both personal well-being and communal harmony. This section delves into the nature of feminine energy, contrasts it with masculine energy, and explores its spiritual significance as advocated by holistic healers like Rachel Rossitto.

1. Defining Feminine Energy:

Feminine energy embodies nurturing, gentleness, intuition, and groundedness. These qualities are crucial for building deep connections, fostering emotional resilience, and maintaining stability. Nurturing promotes growth and potential, while gentleness, often misunderstood as weakness, is a powerful force for resilience and openness. Intuition provides insights beyond rational thought, and groundedness helps maintain balance and connection to core values.

2. Contrasting with Masculine Energy:

Masculine energy, characterized by protectiveness, rationality, and focus, prioritizes doing and achieving. Protectiveness ensures safety and provision, rationality supports objective decision-making, and focus drives goal attainment. These traits are essential for progress and efficiency but need to be balanced by the receptive and nurturing aspects of feminine energy to avoid a lopsided approach to life.

3. Spiritual and Healing Aspects:

Holistic healer Rachel Rossitto highlights the spiritual importance of feminine energy in personal and communal healing. It connects us to life's profound mysteries and enables a holistic approach that integrates emotional and spiritual experiences. This sacred energy is crucial for healing, offering a pathway to a balanced life and helping rectify societal imbalances caused by the undervaluation of feminine traits.

4. Personal and Communal Healing

The integration of feminine energy into daily life can profoundly impact personal health and communal interactions. For individuals, engaging more deeply with their feminine side can lead to enhanced self-awareness, greater emotional resilience, and a more meaningful spiritual life.

In communities, increased feminine energy can foster greater cooperation, deeper understanding between members, and a more compassionate approach to communal challenges.

Reclaiming the Divine Feminine

Embracing feminine energy in traditionally masculine settings is both challenging and transformative. Rachel Rossitto's work with leaders showcases the significant benefits of integrating this energy into professional leadership practices. Here is how;

1. Rachel Rossitto's Approach to Feminine Energy

Rachel Rossitto, a holistic healer, has dedicated her career to helping individuals, particularly women in leadership roles, to embrace and integrate feminine energy into their lives. Her approach involves coaching sessions that focus on self-awareness and balance.

These sessions emphasize the strategic use of feminine traits. Traits such as empathy, intuition, and collaborative leadership are central to her teachings. These sessions are tailored to help leaders understand and leverage these qualities not just for personal growth but also for enhancing their professional effectiveness.

2. Integration in Corporate and Community Leadership

Rossitto's work extends into the corporate world, where she engages with executives and teams to foster environments that value and incorporate feminine energies. She assists leaders in recognizing the importance of nurturing qualities. She also highlights the role of intuitive decision-making.

Additionally, she emphasizes the strength of vulnerability in building strong, resilient teams. For community leaders, her focus is on creating inclusive spaces that prioritize collective well-being and empathy, which are essential for sustainable community development.

3. Challenges in Masculine-Dominated Domains

One of the major challenges in reclaiming feminine energy lies in overcoming the entrenched stereotypes and biases in traditionally masculine domains such as corporate leadership and entrepreneurship. Feminine qualities are often undervalued in settings that favor decisiveness, competition, and emotional detachment.

These masculine traits are wrongly equated with professional competence. Leaders working to integrate feminine energy must navigate skepticism and sometimes outright resistance, both from peers and subordinates.

4. Transformations and Impact

The transformations witnessed by those who successfully integrate feminine energy into their leadership styles are significant. Leaders report better team dynamics, increased creativity, and higher levels of employee satisfaction and engagement.

On a personal level, leaders find that embracing their full spectrum of energies not only enhances their professional life but also leads to a more fulfilled, balanced personal life. The acknowledgment and valuation of feminine energy also pave the way for more women and men to express their authentic selves, contributing to a shift in organizational cultures and societal norms.

Practical Applications and Daily Rituals

Integrating and honoring feminine energy daily enhances personal growth and spiritual fulfillment. Here are effective ways to connect with your feminine side:

- **Morning Rituals:** Begin the day with grounding practices such as meditation, deep breathing, or gentle stretching to set a mindful and empowered tone. Personalizing these rituals makes them a cherished part of your morning.

- **Creating a Personal Sanctuary:** Establish a dedicated space for meditation and reflection, which can range from a simple quiet corner to a more elaborate setup with cushions and calming elements. For frequent travelers, a portable kit with meditation essentials ensures the continuation of this practice anywhere.

- **Journaling and Tea Rituals:** Combine journaling with a tea ritual to foster tranquility and mindfulness. This practice aids in mental clarity and emotional processing, making it easier to navigate daily challenges.

- **Meditation and Breathing Exercises:** Engage in meditation and focused breathing exercises to enhance mindfulness and manage stress. Even short sessions of five to ten minutes can significantly impact emotional and spiritual health, especially for beginners.

Community and Collective Healing

Embracing feminine energy extends beyond individual practices into the realm of community interaction and collective healing. Communities focused on feminine energy practices, like The Wild Collective, play a pivotal role in supporting and nurturing these energies among their members.

1. The Role of Supportive Communities

Communities like The Wild Collective facilitate the growth and expression of feminine energy through shared experiences, rituals, and discussions. These groups provide a safe space where members can explore their spirituality, vulnerability, and strength without judgment.

By participating in such communities, individuals find empowerment in collective acceptance and encouragement, which reinforces their personal journey towards embracing feminine qualities.

2. Impact on Societal Change

Engaging in communities focused on feminine energy does more than support individual growth; it also acts as a catalyst for societal change. As more individuals embrace and express their feminine qualities, such as empathy, nurturing, and collaboration, these traits become more valued across societal structures.

This shift can lead to the dismantling of outdated gender norms, promoting a more inclusive understanding of strength and leadership that values emotional intelligence as highly as rational decision-making.

3. Contributions to Dismantling Gender Norms

The collective embrace of feminine energy in community settings challenges the traditional binary norms of gender. It shows that traits traditionally labeled as 'feminine' are valuable and effective in various contexts, including leadership and decision-making.

As communities like The Wild Collective grow and gain visibility, they challenge and change the broader cultural narratives around gender, making it more acceptable and desirable for all individuals, regardless of gender, to express and value these traits.

Reflection Questions And Action Steps

To enhance your understanding and integration of feminine energy, this section provides targeted reflection questions and practical action steps.

Reflection Questions

1. How do I express nurturing, intuition, and empathy in my life?

Consider how these traits influence your decisions and interactions.

2. Where might I be suppressing my feminine energy?

Identify situations or relationships where you restrain these qualities.

3. What barriers exist to embracing my feminine side?

Reflect on societal or personal obstacles.

4. How do I perceive feminine qualities in others?

Evaluate whether you see these traits as strengths or weaknesses.

Action Steps

- **Establish a Daily Ritual:** Incorporate a simple routine like meditation, journaling, or yoga to connect with your feminine energy.

- **Create a Personal Sanctuary:** Set up a dedicated space at home for activities that nurture your feminine side.

- **Join a Community:** Connect with groups that focus on developing feminine energy, such as The Wild Collective.

- **Educate Yourself and Others:** Learn more about feminine energy and share your insights to broaden understanding.

- **Reflect Regularly:** Dedicate time each week to assess your progress and adjust your practices as needed.

Summary:

The journey to embracing feminine energy is not merely a path to personal fulfillment—it is a revolutionary act that challenges outdated norms and paves the way for a more inclusive and equitable society. By recognizing and nurturing both the feminine and masculine within us, we not only achieve a more balanced life but also contribute to the collective evolution of our understanding of human potential.

WOMEN IN SOCIAL MEDIA

Women and Social Media: A Cesspool of Negativity and Judgment

In today's digital age, social media has become an inescapable part of our lives. Platforms like Face book, Twitter, and Instagram allow us to connect with friends, share updates, and stay informed about the world around us. However, beneath the surface of these seemingly harmless networks lies a dark undercurrent of negativity, judgment, and outright hatred, particularly towards women.

The Statistics: A Sobering Reality

The numbers speak for themselves. According to a recent study by the Pew Research Center, nearly four in ten women have experienced online harassment, with 27%reporting outright stalking or sexual harassment. Even more alarming, the study found that women are twice as likely as men to view online harassment as a significant problem.

But the issue goes beyond mere harassment. Women on social media are routinely subjected to a barrage of unsolicited opinions, judgments, and downright abuse, often from other women. It's a toxic environment where every aspect of a woman's life is dissected, criticized, and deemed either acceptable or unacceptable by strangers.

The Case of Nelly and Ashanti: A Microcosm of the Problem

The recent news of rapper Nelly and singer Ashanti expecting their first child together has unleashed a torrent of negative comments, judgments, and unsolicited advice from social media users. Despite the joyous occasion, the couple has been met with a deluge of opinions ranging from whether Nelly should marry Ashanti to criticisms about their ages (Ashanti is 43) and the timing of their parenthood.

A glance at the comments section on any news article or social media post about the couple reveals a cesspool of negativity, with people who have no personal connection to Nelly or Ashanti feeling entitled to weigh in on the most intimate aspects of their lives.

"She's too old to be having her first child."

"He needs to put a ring on it."

"They're just looking for attention."

The comments are endless, and they all share a common thread: the belief that these strangers have the right to pass judgment on two consenting adults and their personal life choices.

The Roots of the Problem: Why Women Tear Each Other Down

So, why are women so quick to tear each other down on social media? The roots of this issue are complex and multifaceted, but a few key factors stand out.

- a) **Internalized Misogyny:** From a young age, women are conditioned to believe that their worth is intrinsically tied to their appearance, relationships, and adherence to societal norms. This internalized misogyny often manifests as a need to criticize and judge other women in an attempt to validate one's own choices and perceived superiority.

b) **Jealousy and Insecurity:** Social media has a way of amplifying feelings of inadequacy and in security. When we see others living seemingly perfect lives, it can trigger feelings of jealousy and resentment, which often spill over into the form of negative comments and judgments.

c) **Anonymity and Lack of Accountability:** The anonymity afforded by social media platforms can encourage people to say things they would never dream of uttering in person. Without the fear of consequences or accountability, some users feel emboldened to unleash their most toxic thoughts and opinions on others.

The Consequences: A Perpetuation of Negativity and Self-Hate

The consequences of this endless cycle of negativity and judgment are far-reaching and insidious. Not only does it perpetuate a culture of misogyny and self-hate among women, but it also has the potential to inflict actual emotional harm on those on the receiving end.

Imagine being Ashanti or Nelly, excited about starting a new chapter in their lives as parents, only to be bombarded with a tidal wave of negativity and unsolicited opinions from strangers. How demoralizing and hurtful must that feel?

But the impact extends far beyond just celebrities. Every day, women from all walks of life are subjected to this same level of judgment and negativity on social media simply for daring to live their lives on their terms.

The Time for Change: Reclaiming Social Media as a Positive Space

So, what can be done to reclaim social media as a positive, uplifting space for women? The solution lies in a collective effort to challenge internalized misogyny, cultivate empathy, and practice mindfulness when engaging with others online.

Challenge Internalized Misogyny: The first step is to acknowledge and actively work to dismantle the internalized misogyny that drives so much of the negativity and judgment directed at other women. This means consciously rejecting societal norms that seek to pit women against each other and embracing a mindset of solidarity and support.

Cultivate Empathy: Before hitting that "post" button, take a moment to consider the impact your words might have on the person on the receiving end. Imagine how you would feel if someone said the same thing about you oral loved one. Empathy is a powerful antidote to negativity and judgment.

Practice Mindfulness: If you find yourself compelled to leave a negative comment or judgment on someone's social media post, pause and ask yourself, "Is this truly my business?" Chances are, if it doesn't directly impact your life, it's best to keep scrolling and mind your affairs.

Lead by Example: Be the change you wish to see on social media. Use your platform to spread positivity, uplift others, and model the kind of behavior you want to see from others.

The Power of Positivity: Investing Time in Personal Growth

Instead of investing time and energy into judging and criticizing others, imagine the personal growth and fulfillment that could come from redirecting that energy toward positive pursuits. Whether it's working towards a personal goal, learning a new skill, or simply cultivating more self-love and acceptance, the time spent scrolling and leaving negative comments could be better spent on activities that enrich your life and those around you.

The truth is, the negative comments and judgments we leave on social media say far more about us than they do about the person we're criticizing. They reveal our insecurities, jealousies, and unhappiness with ourselves. By choosing to spread positivity and mind our own business, we not only create a better online environment for all, but we also free ourselves from the shackles of negativity that hold us back from proper personal growth and fulfillment.

The Choice is Ours: Uplift or Tear Down?

In the end, the choice is ours. We can continue to perpetuate the cycle of negativity, judgment, and hatred that plagues social media, or we can choose to be agents of change, uplifting and supporting one another as women.

The path forward is clear: let's reclaim social media as a space of positivity, empathy, and personal growth. Let's celebrate each other's triumphs, offer support during struggles, and above all, mind our own business when it comes to the individual lives and choices of others.

After all, when we lift each other, we rise together.

The Real Story behind the Images

Decoding Beauty Ideals: Social Media Vs. Reality

Social media sites like Face book and Instagram have influenced numerous people's lives. It is crucial to determine if using social media affects one's self-concept, self-esteem, body image, and body dissatisfaction since adults - particularly women - are the main users of such platforms. Researchers have begun objectively studying, and recent research has produced contradictory findings. With an emphasis on Instagram, Face book, and other well-known image - based platforms, the current article tries to analyze these data. It presents potential reasons for the impacts of social media usage on body dissatisfaction.

Essena O'Neill, a 19-year-old Australian Internet sensation who deserted social media in November 2015 to demonstrate that social media is only a vehicle for fraudulent self-promotion, said, "Social media is not real life. "With more than 600,000 followers on Instagram alone, Essena was a popular user of the social media sites Instagram, Tumblr, YouTube, and others. Her supporters and friends erupted in a commotion as soon as she stopped speaking. They confronted the Australian adolescent and said she had purposefully deleted her social media accounts to get more notoriety and attention. Following Essena's decision to stop using social media, her friends, admirers, and followers started uploading blogs and videos; some even sent death threats.

Interviews conducted with women about their social media experiences and self-esteem during the same period Essena O'Neill withdrew from Instagram revealed common feelings of insecurity, aligning with O'Neill's observations. Many participants expressed concerns over the number of "likes" they received, apprehension about not appearing attractive in their photos, fear of being perceived differently online versus in real life, and anxiety over which aspects of their lives would attract attention. The process of selecting the perfect photo, editing it, and frequently checking for updates on "likes" exacerbated these insecurities. Despite recognizing these patterns, many found it challenging to alter their behaviors, driven by the desire to conform within the social media landscape. A significant number confessed to living virtually online, placing immense value on their digital persona. This preoccupation with social media has been suggested as a contributing factor to body dissatisfaction, though research findings on the relationship between social media use and body image concerns remain inconclusive.

The Impact of the Media

The use of social media, in particular, has grown significantly during the last ten years and is still growing. In 2015, according to Pew Research Centre, 71% of 13 to 17-year-olds used Facebook, 52% used Instagram, and 41% used Snapchat. Adolescent girls and women's self-confidence and body satisfaction may suffer due to this rise in social media use, particularly on Facebook and Instagram.

According to some experts, women exposed to fashion periodicals or television programs are likelier to have eating disorders and body dissatisfaction. These studies examined media exposure and body image to demonstrate a potential connection between seeing slim bodies in the media and feeling unsatisfied with one's body.

The researchers examined whether exposure to mass media (such as television, videos, CD players, MP3 players, internet access, and mobile phone access) directly and indirectly was linked to eating disorders in females from Fiji. They discovered links between eating disorders in Fijian females and direct mass media exposure (i.e, personal media exposure) and indirect mass media exposure (i.e, media exposure to persons in one's peer group).

Despite its shortcomings, namely the uncertainty around the general ability of the results. The research contends that social networks, at least in this instance, were crucial to the association between media and eating disorders, which may also include a link between media and body dissatisfaction.

However, these results must be tempered because other studies have yet to discover a connection between watching image-based media and body dissatisfaction. Surprisingly, the study found that women reported feeling better about their bodies after seeing photographs of overweight people but had no change in perception of their bodies after seeing images of skinny people. These results raise questions about the possible connection between media and body image, pointing to the need for more research.

Use of Social Media

A collaborative platform for social contact between what seems like a limitless number of individuals is provided by social media. The regular usage of social media platforms has been linked to several advantages. "The six key overarching benefits were identified as (1) increased interactions with others, (2) more available, shared, and tailored information, (3) increased accessibility and widening access to health information, (4) peer, social, emotional support, (5) public health surveillance, and (6) potential to influence health policy" Social media, especially image-based social media, has many advantages, but there is also certain usage of these platforms that might have unintended consequences. This analysis primarily examines Pinterest, Instagram, and Facebook as image-based social media sites.

Insatiable With Your Body on Instagram

There are a variety of factors that contribute to Instagram's detrimental impact on women. It may leave a permanent, emotional, and mental scar, contributing to various mental health problems.

Low self-esteem is mediated by anxiety and sadness. Low self-esteem may result from various factors, with social media like Instagram playing a significant role. The promotion of a false sense of self on Instagram leads to self-criticism. By altering their bodies to reflect society's ideals of feminine beauty, Instagram models and influencers profit from these experiences and increase their fame on social media. In keeping with the first argument in favor, it is clear that to be on Instagram, a person must be "beautiful" in the eyes of society and be able to buy costly goods. Luxury vehicles, high-end clothing labels, and enormous mansions are rare. The average individual may put forth much effort and savings and not achieve their goals. Instagram gives the impression that obtaining these goods is simple. Because not everyone can afford costly material items, this may lead to poor self-esteem and a fear of missing out.

Physical characteristics might contribute to women's self-hatred in addition to monetary items. Trends may have an impact on this. Inspiration, often known as "fitspo" is a widespread trend wherein beauty influencers flaunt their fitness objectives and results by publishing pictures of their bodies. Because pictures of other people are continually being shared online, as was previously said, it is simple to compare what you have to what others have. These fitness influencers are unaware of the potential detrimental effects of their material, particularly when it is unrealistic. For instance, a lady can follow the same fitness routine and consume the same foods yet still need to meet the standards set by a beauty influencer. This is because of Instagram's deceit and how simple it is to conceal using an angle or filter. In addition to this, each person has a unique physical makeup, including a unique bodily structure and metabolism. If an influencer changes their photographs, viewers can only accomplish the same result, which may make them feel defeated. One report shows that sadness and anxiety may directly correlate with poor self-esteem. Examining the root causes of poor self-esteem supports the claim that Instagram encourages unrealistic expectations.

Using social media tools to keep in touch and remain current is referred to as social networking. The most popular media-sharing platforms are Facebook, Instagram, and Twitter. They all adhere to the same norms of conduct and regulations inside a social networking community. This foundation may make people feel out of place in their social circle. When it comes to feminine beauty standards, this is very evident. Body hair and body shaming are two topics that are quite divisive. As women develop into their bodies and their body hair, in particular, becomes more noticeable, this has an influence on them. Anyone may publicly express their thoughts, which is problematic since this information is usually false.

4 Strategies for Creating a Positive Connection with Oneself

What if you wish to strengthen your connection with yourself or do not have one? Here are four methods to help you get along with yourself better.

1. Develop a Constructive Internal Discourse You have what is known as an "inner dialogue" with yourself all day long

A constructive or healthy internal conversation promotes self-assurance and helps overcome anxiety and despair. Negative thoughts or increased emotions of shame may result from an improper internal conversation. Consider paying attention to how you converse with yourself during the day to foster a positive inner conversation. Your kindness? Do you place more emphasis on events that go well or those that go wrong?

Next, try to focus on being grateful. You may cultivate a general thankfulness practice by concentrating on your life's positive aspects. It is normal for worrying or pessimistic thoughts to sometimes surface. It could be beneficial to hunt for proof to disprove your pessimistic beliefs.

2. Think About Listing Your Opportunities and Talents

Putting a value on your advantages might boost your self-assurance. Being kind and patient with oneself may be easier if you acknowledge that you have room for improvement.

Consider compiling a list of your advantages. If you find this difficult, think about asking your loving friends and relatives what they think you are capable of. You might also get assistance from a mentor, life coach, or mental health specialist in figuring out your special qualities and how to work on acquiring new talents.

3. Time Alone May Be Beneficial

You might make room for self-reflection and inner work with alone time.

Consider concentrating on discovering your.

- Fundamental convictions

- Favors and disfavors
- Contemporary difficulties
- Aims in life

Everyone's idea of alone time may be different.

You may take an hour-long coffee break, a lengthy bath, or a stroll. Youmay decide not to bring a buddy to a sports event. You may listen to your favorite podcast while doing mindless housework.

4. Try To Attend to Your Requirements

You must learn to love yourself to have a good connection with yourself and others. Start by taking care of yourself.

What would self-awareness look like?

- Consuming nutrient-rich food
- Participating in physical activities
- Enhancing good sleep habits
- Getting a new job or attending a course
- Interacting with family and friends
- Journaling
- Using relaxation methods
- Obtaining expert assistance.

8

SEXUAL WELLNESS AND WELL BEING

The Importance of Sex

Sexuality is an intrinsic aspect of human existence, influencing not only our physical bodies but also our emotions, relationships, and overall well-being. From the earliest stages of human development to the twilight years of life, sexuality plays a pivotal role in shaping our experiences and interactions with the world around us. In this chapter, we explore the multifaceted importance of sex and its profound impact on various aspects of human life.

Biological Imperatives

At its core, sex serves as the mechanism for procreation, ensuring the continuation of the human species. Through sexual reproduction, genetic material is passed down from one generation to the next, perpetuating the diversity of life on Earth. These biological imperative underscores the fundamental importance of sex in the perpetuation of life itself.

Emotional Connection

Beyond its reproductive function, sex plays a crucial role in fostering emotional intimacy and connection between individuals. The physical act of sexual intercourse releases a cascade of hormones, including oxytocin and dopamine, which are associated with feelings of bonding, trust, and pleasure. These neurochemicals not only deepen emotional bonds between partners but also contribute to overall feelings of well-being and happiness.

Self-Expression and Identity

Sexuality is an integral part of our identity, shaping how we perceive ourselves and interact with others. Our sexual preferences, desires, and behaviors are deeply intertwined with our sense of self, influencing everything from our personal relationships to our cultural and social identities. By embracing and expressing our sexuality authentically, we affirm our individuality and celebrate the diversity of human experience.

Health and Wellness

Numerous studies have shown that regular sexual activity is associated with various health benefits, both physical and psychological. From boosting the immune system and improving cardiovascular health to reducing stress and alleviating symptoms of depression, sex has been shown to have a positive impact on overall well-being. Furthermore, sexual satisfaction and fulfillment are essential components of a healthy and fulfilling life.

Social and Cultural Significance

Sexuality is not only a deeply personal experience but also a social and cultural phenomenon that shapes societies and influences norms and values. Throughout history, attitudes toward sex have varied widely across different cultures and time periods, reflecting broader social and religious beliefs, moral codes, and political ideologies. Understanding the cultural context of sexuality is crucial for navigating social expectations and fostering inclusive and respectful attitudes toward diverse expressions of human sexuality.

In conclusion, the importance of sex extends far beyond its biological function, encompassing emotional, social, and cultural dimensions. From fostering emotional connection and self-expression to promoting health and well-being, sexuality influences virtually every aspect of human life. By recognizing and embracing the significance of sex, we can cultivate healthier relationships, promote sexual wellness, and create a more inclusive and understanding society. In the subsequent chapters of this comprehensive guide, we will delve deeper into the various facets of sexuality and explore practical strategies for enhancing sexual health and fulfillment.

Why is Sex Important?

Sexuality is a fundamental aspect of human existence, deeply intertwined with our physical, emotional, and social well-being. But why exactly is sex so important in our lives? In this chapter, we will explore the myriad reasons why sex matters and the profound impact it has on various aspects of human life.

Intimacy and Connection

One of the primary reasons why sex is important is its ability to foster intimacy and connection between individuals. The physical act of sexual intercourse releases a cocktail of hormones, including oxytocin and dopamine, which are known as the "bonding hormones." These chemicals play a crucial role in strengthening emotional bonds between partners, deepening feelings of trust, love, and intimacy.

Emotional Well-Being

Sexual activity has been linked to improved emotional well-being and mental health. Studies have shown that regular sexual activity can reduce symptoms of anxiety and depression, alleviate stress, and promote overall feelings of happiness and satisfaction. The release of endorphins during sex produces a natural high, boosting mood and creating a sense of euphoria and relaxation.

Physical Health Benefits

Engaging in sexual activity has numerous physical health benefits as well. From boosting the immune system and improving cardiovascular health to reducing the risk of certain cancers and enhancing longevity, sex has been shown to have a positive impact on overall health and wellness. Regular sexual activity is also associated with lower blood pressure, improved sleep quality, and even pain relief.

Relationship Satisfaction

Sexual satisfaction is a key component of relationship satisfaction. Couples who engage in regular sexual activity tend to report higher levels of relationship satisfaction and intimacy compared to those who do not. Sex helps to strengthen the emotional bond between partners, enhance communication and trust, and promote feelings of closeness and connection.

Self-Expression and Identity

Sexuality is an integral part of our identity, allowing us to express ourselves authentically and explore our desires and preferences. By embracing our sexuality, we affirm our individuality and celebrate the diversity of human experience. Sexuality is a deeply personal aspect of who we are, and expressing it freely contributes to our overall sense of self and well-being.

Pleasure and Enjoyment

Perhaps most importantly, sex is important because it brings pleasure and enjoyment into our lives. The physical sensations and emotional connection experienced during sex can be intensely pleasurable and fulfilling. Whether with a partner or through solo exploration, sex provides an opportunity to experience pleasure, satisfaction, and joy.

sex is important for a multitude of reasons, ranging from its ability to foster intimacy and connection to its positive impact on physical and emotional well-being. By recognizing the importance of sex in our lives, we can cultivate heal their relationships, promote sexual wellness, and enhance overall quality of life. In the subsequent chapters of this comprehensive guide, we will delve deeper into the various aspects of sexuality and explore practical strategies for enhancing sexual health and fulfillment.

Sex in Your 50s

As individuals enter their 50s and beyond, there can be a common misconception that sexual activity diminishes or becomes less important. However, contrary to popular belief, many people find that their sexual experiences and desires continue to evolve and thrive during this stage of life. In this chapter, we will explore the dynamics of sex in your 50s and discuss how individuals can navigate this period to maintain a fulfilling and satisfying sex life.

Embracing Change

One of the key aspects of sex in your 50s is embracing the changes that naturally occur with age. Both men and women may experience physiological changes, such as decreased hormone levels, changes in libido, and alterations in sexual function. It's essential to recognize that these changes are a normal part of the aging process and do not necessarily signify the end of sexual activity.

Communication and Connection

Maintaining open and honest communication with your partner is crucial for navigating sex in your 50s. As bodies and desires evolve, it's essential to discuss any concerns or preferences openly and respectfully. Building emotional intimacy and connection through communication can enhance sexual satisfaction and promote a deeper sense of intimacy between partners.

Exploring New Horizons

Entering your 50s can be an opportunity to explore new aspects of your sexuality and experiment with different forms of intimacy. Whether it's trying new positions, incorporating sensual massage, or exploring erotic fantasies, embracing novelty and adventure can reignite passion and excitement in the bedroom.

Prioritizing Sexual Health

As individuals age, prioritizing sexual health becomes increasingly important. This includes regular check-ups with healthcare providers to address any concerns related to sexual function or reproductive health. Additionally, practicing safe sex and taking preventative measures against sexually transmitted infections (STIs) remains crucial for maintaining sexual well-being.

Redefining Intimacy

In your 50s, intimacy extends beyond physical closeness to encompass emotional connection, trust, and mutual understanding. Investing time and effort into nurturing these aspects of intimacy can enhance sexual satisfaction and fulfillment, even as physical capabilities may change with age.

Embracing Sensuality

Sensuality plays a significant role in sexual experiences at any age but can take on added importance in your 50s. Engaging in activities that stimulate the senses, such as candlelit dinners, romantic getaways, or sensual massages, can enhance arousal and deepen emotional connection between partners.

Seeking Support

If individuals encounter challenges or concerns related to sex in their 50s, seeking support from healthcare professionals or qualified therapists can be beneficial. There are numerous resources available, including sexual health clinics, couples counseling, and educational materials, designed to address the unique needs and experiences of individuals in this stage of life.

sex in your 50s offers opportunities for growth, exploration, and connection. By embracing change, prioritizing communication, and nurturing intimacy, individual scan continue to enjoy fulfilling and satisfying sexual experiences well into their later years. In the subsequent chapters of this comprehensive guide, we will delve deeper into specific aspects of sexual health and wellness to support individuals in their journey towards sexual fulfillment.

Explaining What Sex Is

Sex is a complex and multifaceted aspect of human experience that extends far beyond the act of intercourse. In this chapter, we will explore the diverse dimensions of sex, from its biological foundations to its emotional and social significance. By expanding our understanding of what sex entails, we can appreciate the richness and diversity of human sexuality.

Beyond Intercourse

While intercourse is often the first thing that comes to mind when we think of sex, it's essential to recognize that sex encompasses a wide range of activities beyond penetrative intercourse. This includes kissing, touching, oral sex, mutual masturbation, and other forms of intimate contact that can bring pleasure and satisfaction to individuals and couples.

Physical Pleasure

At its core, sex is about experiencing physical pleasure and arousal. The human body is equipped with a variety of erogenous zones, including the genitals, lips, nipples, and other sensitive areas, which can be stimulated to elicit pleasurable sensations. Exploring these sensations and learning how to pleasure oneself and one's partner is an integral part of sexual experience.

Emotional Connection

Sex is not just about physical sensations; it also involves emotional connection and intimacy between partners. The bond formed during sexual activity releases hormones like oxytocin, often referred to as the "love hormone," which promotes feelings of closeness, trust, and affection.

Sharing intimacy with a partner can deepen emotional connection and strengthen the bond between individuals.

Consent and Communication

Central to a healthy and fulfilling sexual experience is the concept of consent and open communication. Consent means that all parties involved freely and enthusiastically agree to engage in sexual activity, without coercion or pressure. Effective communication about desires, boundaries, and preferences ensures that everyone involved feels respected and valued, fostering trust and intimacy in the relationship.

Pleasure and Satisfaction

Sexual pleasure and satisfaction are subjective experiences that vary from person to person. What feels pleasurable for one individual may not be enjoyable for another. It's essential for individuals and couples to explore their own desires and preferences and communicate openly with their partners about what brings them pleasure and satisfaction.

Connection to Identity

Sexuality is an integral part of human identity and self-expression. Our sexual preferences, desires, and behaviors play a significant role in shaping who we are and how we relate to others. Embracing and accepting our sexuality allows us to affirm our individuality and celebrate the diversity of human experience.

In conclusion, sex is a rich and multifaceted aspect of human life that encompasses physical pleasure, emotional connection, and self-expression. By expanding our understanding of what sex entails, we can cultivate healthier and more fulfilling sexual experiences and relationships. In the subsequent chapters of this comprehensive guide, we will delve deeper into specific aspects of sexual health and wellness to support individuals in their journey towards sexual fulfillment.

Self-Pleasure Without a Partner

Self-pleasure, often referred to as masturbation, is a natural and healthy aspect of human sexuality. While it may be a topic that is sometimes surrounded by stigma or taboo, self-pleasure plays an essential role in exploring one's own body, understanding one's desires, and experiencing sexual pleasure and satisfaction. In this chapter, we will delve into the importance of self-pleasure and provide guidance on how individuals can engage in solo sexual exploration in a safe and fulfilling manner.

Understanding Self-Pleasure

Self-pleasure involves stimulating one's own body to elicit sexual arousal and pleasure. This can include touching or stroking the genitals, exploring erogenous zones, or using sex toys or other aids to enhance sensation. Masturbation is a normal and healthy part of human sexuality, and individuals of all genders and sexual orientations engage in self-pleasure.

Exploring Desire and Pleasure

Engaging in self-pleasure allows individuals to explore their own desires, preferences, and fantasies without the need for a partner. By experimenting with different techniques and sensations, individuals can learn more about what brings them pleasure and satisfaction, leading to a deeper understanding of their own sexuality.

Stress Relief and Relaxation

Masturbation can also serve as a natural way to relieve stress and tension, promoting relaxation and overall well-being. The release of endorphins during orgasm produces feelings of pleasure and euphoria, which can help to alleviate feelings of anxiety or stress. Taking time for self-pleasure can be a valuable form of self-care and self-soothing.

Sexual Health Benefits

In addition to providing pleasure and relaxation, masturbation offers several potential health benefits. For individuals with vulvas, self-pleasure can help to increase vaginal lubrication and promote pelvic floor muscle tone. For individuals with penises, masturbation can aid in maintaining erectile function and prostate health. Regular masturbation can also help individuals become more familiar with their own bodies, making it easier to detect any changes or abnormalities.

Normalizing Solo Sexual Exploration

It's important to normalize and destigmatize the act of self-pleasure, as it is a natural and healthy aspect of human sexuality. Encouraging open and honest conversations about masturbation can help individuals feel more comfortable exploring their own bodies and desires. By removing the shame or guilt often associated with self-pleasure, individuals can embrace their sexuality more fully and experience greater sexual satisfaction.

Safety and Consent

While self-pleasure is generally safe and healthy, it's essential to practice it in a way that prioritizes safety and consent. This includes using clean hands or sex toys, avoiding excessive or rough stimulation that could cause discomfort or injury, and respecting one's own boundaries and limits. It's also important to recognize that masturbation is a personal choice, and individuals should feel empowered to engage in it only when they feel comfortable and ready.

In conclusion, self-pleasure is a normal and healthy aspect of human sexuality that offers numerous benefits, including exploring desire, relieving stress, and promoting sexual health. By embracing solo sexual exploration without shame or stigma, individuals can enhance their understanding of their own bodies and desires, leading to greater sexual satisfaction and fulfillment. In the subsequent chapters of this comprehensive guide, we will continue to explore various aspects of sexual health and wellness to support individuals in their journey towards sexual fulfillment, whether alone or with a partner.

Understanding Sex Drive

Sex drive, also known as libido, refers to a person's natural inclination or desire for sexual activity. It is a complex phenomenon influenced by a combination of biological, psychological, and social factors. In this chapter, we will explore the intricacies of sex drive, its underlying mechanisms, and the various factors that can influence its intensity and expression.

Biological Basis

Sex drive is rooted in biology, with hormones playing a central role in regulating sexual desire and arousal. Testosterone, often referred to as the "male" hormone, is primarily responsible for stimulating sex drive in both men and women. However, other hormones, such as estrogen and progesterone in women, also contribute to sexual desire and response.

Psychological Factors

In addition to biological influences, psychological factors play a significant role in shaping sex drive. Emotional well-being, stress levels, self-esteem, and relationship satisfaction can all impact a person's libido. For example, individuals experiencing high levels of stress or anxiety may find that their sex drive diminishes, while those in fulfilling and supportive relationships may experience heightened desire.

Social and Cultural Influences

Sex drive is also influenced by social and cultural factors, including societal norms, cultural beliefs, and personal values. Messages about sex and sexuality conveyed by family, peers, media, and society at large can shape an individual's attitudes toward sex and influence their level of desire. Cultural taboos surrounding sex may also impact how individuals express and experience their libido.

Variability and Fluidity

It's important to recognize that sex drive is not static but can vary over time and in different circumstances. Factors such as age, hormonal changes, life events, and health conditions can all influence fluctuations in sex drive. Additionally, individuals may experience changes in their libido in response to specific stimuli or situations, such as being in a new relationship or experiencing a period of emotional distress.

Differences Between Individuals

Sex drive varies widely among individuals and can differ based on factors such as age, gender, sexual orientation, and personal preferences. While some individuals may have a high libido and experience frequent and intense sexual desire, others may have a lower libido and feel less inclined toward sexual activity. These differences are entirely normal and do not necessarily indicate a problem or dysfunction.

Navigating Changes in Sex Drive

As individuals navigate changes in their sex drive, it's essential to approach these fluctuations with patience, understanding, and open communication. If changes in libido are causing distress or dissatisfaction, seeking support from a health care professional or qualified therapist can be helpful. Additionally, exploring strategies to enhance intimacy and connection with a partner can help to reignite desire and promote a satisfying sex life.

In conclusion, sex drive is a complex and multifaceted aspect of human sexuality influenced by biological, psychological, and social factors. By understanding the underlying mechanisms of sex drive and the various factors that can influence its expression, individuals can navigate changes in libido with greater awareness and adaptability. In the subsequent chapters of this comprehensive guide, we will continue to explore various aspects of sexual health and wellness to support individuals in optimizing their sexual experiences and satisfaction.

How Sex Can Improve Daily Life

Sexual activity is not just a pleasurable pastime; it also has numerous benefits that extend beyond the bedroom and can positively impact various aspects of daily life. In this chapter, we will explore the ways in which engaging in regular sexual activity can enhance overall well-being and contribute to a happier, healthier lifestyle.

Stress Reduction

One of the most well-known benefits of sex is its ability to reduce stress levels. Engaging in sexual activity triggers the release of endorphins often referred to as "feel-good" hormones, which promote feelings of relaxation and euphoria. This natural stress relief can help individuals unwind after a long day, alleviate tension, and improve overall mood.

Improved Physical Health

Sexual activity offers several physical health benefits that can contribute to improved overall well-being. Regular sexual activity has been linked to lower blood pressure, improved cardiovascular health, and even enhanced immune function. Additionally, the physical exertion associated with sex can help to burn calories and promote physical fitness.

Enhanced Emotional Bonding

Sexual intimacy fosters emotional connection and bonding between partners. There lease of oxytocin, often called the "love hormone," during sexual activity promotes feelings of trust, intimacy, and affection. Sharing intimate moments with a partner can strengthen the emotional bond between them, leading to greater relationship satisfaction and stability.

Better Sleep Quality

Engaging in sexual activity can also improve sleep quality. The release of endorphins and other neurochemicals during sex promotes relaxation and can help individuals fall asleep more easily. Additionally, the physical and emotional intimacy shared during sexual activity can create a sense of security and comfort, leading to more restful sleep.

Pain Relief

Sexual activity has been shown to have pain-relieving effects, thanks to the release of endorphins and other natural painkillers. For individuals experiencing mild to moderate pain, engaging in sexual activity can provide temporary relief and distraction from discomfort. Additionally, orgasms have been associated with temporary increases in pain tolerance.

Boosted Self-Esteem

Positive sexual experiences can contribute to increased self-esteem and feelings of self-worth. Achieving sexual satisfaction and feeling desired by a partner can bolster confidence and promote a positive self-image. Additionally, the emotional connection and intimacy shared during sex can reinforce feelings of acceptance and validation.

In conclusion, engaging in regular sexual activity can have a range of positive effects on daily life, from reducing stress and improving physical health to enhancing emotional bonding and boosting self-esteem. By prioritizing sexual intimacy and connection, individuals can enjoy the numerous benefits that sex has to offer and cultivate a happier, healthier lifestyle. In the subsequent chapters of this comprehensive guide, we will continue to explore various aspects of sexual health and wellness to support individuals in optimizing their sexual experiences and overall well-being.

Communication About Needs and Desires

Effective communication is the cornerstone of a healthy and satisfying sexual relationship. In this chapter, we will explore the importance of open and honest communication about sexual needs and desires, as well as provide guidance on how to initiate and navigate these crucial conversations with your partner.

Creating a Safe and Trusting Environment

The foundation of productive communication about sexual needs and desires is creating a safe and trusting environment where both partners feel comfortable expressing themselves openly and honestly. This requires mutual respect, empathy, and non-judgmental listening. Establishing trust and emotional intimacy lays the groundwork for meaningful conversations about sexuality.

Identifying and Expressing Needs

Understanding and articulating your own sexual needs is essential for effective communication with your partner. Take time to reflect on what you desire and require in terms of intimacy, pleasure, and satisfaction. Be specific and clear in expressing your needs, using "I" statements to convey your feelings and desires without blaming or criticizing your partner.

Active Listening

In addition to expressing your own needs, it's crucial to listen actively and attentive to your partner's needs and desires. Practice empathetic listening, seeking to understand their perspective without interrupting or judging. Validate their feelings and experiences, and show genuine interest in meeting their needs and desires.

Discussing Boundaries and Consent

Communication about sexual needs and desires should also encompass discussions about boundaries and consent. Clearly establish and respect each other's boundaries, and ensure that any sexual activity is consensual and mutually desired.

Check in with your partner regularly to ensure ongoing consent and comfort.

Addressing Challenges and Concerns

Effective communication involves addressing challenges and concerns openly and constructively. If issues arise in your sexual relationship, approach them with empathy and willingness to problem-solve together. Avoid placing blame or becoming defensive, and focus on finding mutually beneficial solutions.

Prioritizing Emotional Connection

Remember that communication about sexual needs and desires is not just about physical pleasure; it's also about deepening emotional connection and intimacy with your partner. Share your vulnerabilities, fears, and desires openly, and encourage your partner to do the same. Building emotional intimacy strengthens the bond between partners and enhances sexual satisfaction.

In conclusion, open and honest communication about sexual needs and desires is essential for fostering a healthy and satisfying sexual relationship. By creating a safe and trusting environment, identifying and expressing needs, actively listening to your partner, discussing boundaries and consent, addressing challenges, and prioritizing emotional connection, you can cultivate a relationship that is fulfilling both inside and outside the bedroom. In the subsequent chapters of this comprehensive guide, we will continue to explore various aspects of sexual health and wellness to support individuals and couples in their journey towards sexual fulfillment and satisfaction.

Research suggests that sexual activity can indeed contribute to overall happiness and well-being, particularly for women. Multiple studies have found that women who engage in regular sexual activity report higher levels of life satisfaction, happiness, and emotional well-being compared to those who are less sexually active. One possible explanation is the release of endorphins and oxytocin during sexual activity, which can promote feelings of pleasure, relaxation, and emotional connection.

NAVIGATING MENOPAUSE WITH SELF-LOVE:
A Comprehensive Guide for Women

Introduction:

Menopause is a major hormonal transition in a woman her life, constituting a milestone symbolizing the end of her child bearing period and introduction of the next chapter. Said to be the suspension of menstruation for 12 months minimum, the menopause commonly ensues in women who are aged 45 to 55 (Mayo Clinic, 2022). The natural body process is taking place alongside the decrease in egg production, which is accompanied by the loss of estrogen and progesterone hormone levels that to a significant extent result in physical and emotional changes Although the menopause as a whole is a phenomenon strictly for the females, the route across this stage could be as different as the fingerprints.

Defining Menopause:

Menopause as a whole is a multi-component phenomenon involving physiologically, psychologically, and socially issues. At the biological level, menopause is a condition of gradually lowering of the ovaries production of estrogen and progesterone, finalizing with the ending of menstruation. Women who are in menopause all go through a hormonal phase that can lead to a plethora of symptoms such as hot flashes, night sweats, vaginal dryness, mood swings, and changes in sexual interest (North American Menopause Society, 2022). But, the fact must be taken into consideration that menopause is not indeed the bathroom of just a plethora of symptoms, it is instead the last stage of a woman's life cycle, denoting the ending of an ability to reproduce.

Understanding the Why:

The menopause process mainly occurs due to the aging process as the ovaries of women are not able to respond similarly to hormonal signals as in the peak reproductive time of their lives. In this process the creation of estrogens of channeling of the progesterone is influenced which creates a low level of estrogen in the reproductive cycle and in the menopause as well. While genetics, reproductive background, and lifestyle play a vital role in determining when and how menopause will happen, there are modifiable factors that can affect the timing and personally experienced symptoms of menopause (Harvard Health Publishing, 2021). On the other hand, female patients who have undergone chemotherapy or surgical procedures, like ovariectomy, may experience menopause symptoms earlier. Moreover, lifestyle factors such as smoking, over-imbibing alcohol, and poor diets can aggravate the menopausal effects.

Nurturing Self-Love Through Menopause:

The self-love is a strong life-ocean that teaches us to rise above the hurdles and to embrace the changes of menopause feeling amazing and confident. Growing up loving yourself means seeing yourself with recognition of your worth, as well as in acknowledgment of your needs and always setting boundaries for yourself. Women going through menopause go through a wide range of physical and emotional alterations which the influence their perception of themselves as well as their level of confidence and wellness. The self-love concept allows women to do what needs to be done first and then, enjoy self-care activities that can contribute to their welfare spirit, body, and mind.

Self-love during menopause may seem to manifest through self-care in a particular way. This means weave in actions that build and heal the whole, that is, the body, mind and spirit. For instance, people can improve their condition by performing exercise routine, such as yoga, walking, or swimming thereby solving the symptoms of menopause like hot flashes, weight's gain, and mood changes. However, this kind of exercise is also an aid to health and emotional wellness (Auerbach et al., 2019). Meanwhile, being composed using mindfulness meditation or slow breathing technique can lead to stress reduction as well as general relaxation (Brotto et al, 2018).

Menopause and Self-Love: Mental Health toll:

The real effects of menopause on the woman's mental health and self-worth cannot be emphasized enough. The hormonal fluctuations and the number of menopause physical symptoms may imply mood swing, irritability and depression. That may affect anxiety and depression. Besides, mental health issues arise because women have to deal with such psychological consequences such as loss of their fertility and the positive perception of themselves.

Infusing self-love concepts as part of everyday routine can play an important role in minimizing the negative impacts and providing the psychological relief. For instance, self-compassion training is composed of three components which a person can use regularly, even during difficult times as long as the individual assesses their emotional state correctly (Neff, 2003). Through practicing self-acceptance, women can discover and recognize their own sentiments which will ultimately make way for self-compassion. In the face of menopausal hardships, this might lead to an increase in acceptance of the situations and an improvement of resilience.

Furthermore, consulting our family or friends that may form substituents to our emotions may also be a fantastic source of information and motivation for us during menopause. Having the opportunity to exchange narratives as well as to engage with others who are concurrently going through this transition period can create a sense of not being isolated and instead feeling more energized about loving themselves, unreservedly in the current state of life.

Empowering Self-Care Practices:

Besides emotional support, the adoption of healthy lifestyle routines is as well vitally important in managing the natural symptoms of menopause and maintaining a good well being. Balanced diet which comprises of fruits, vegetables, whole grains, and lean proteins can provide some nutrients and level out hormonal changes brought about by menopause (American Heart Association, 2022). Another foundational dietary element is the inclusion of foods that contain high levels of phytoestrogens, including soybeans, flaxseeds and chickpeas, which in turn can help provide relief from common symptoms like hot flashes, night sweats, among others (Messina et al., 2016).

Practicing exercise is another crucial piece for women at menopause as there are plenty of physical as well as psychological advantages that are in the offer. Cardiovascular circulation and mood can be aided by aerobic activities like walking, running and riding a bike (an example would be "Sternfeld et al., 2014"). Their sleep quality also improves in these aerobic activities. On the flip side, workout routines that are resistance-based help reduce the loss of muscle mass and bones density, which be as a result of hormonal alterations associated with menopause (Kohrt et al., 2019).

Furthermore, the use of some natural supplements and alternative treatments is believed to powerful enough to eliminate menopausal discomfort. In other words, supplements of calcium and vitamin D decrease the risk of osteoporosis and this group of compounds might be prescribed for people who have or are prone to this disease (Weaver et al., 2016). The usage of some botanical remedies, namely black cohosh, evening primrose oil, and red clover, aimed at reducing hot flashes and other menopausal symptoms is possible; however a majority scientific research is still required to guarantee their effectiveness and safety (Dodinet.al, 2013).

Embracing the Journey:

Menopause should no longer be treated as a disease but a normal stage in a woman's life to be respected and celebrated with they way one accepts oneself. Through self-love promotion via self-care routines, emotional support and healthy way of life, women have the ability to glide through adverse times of menopause with dignity, calm and power. They should accept this transition period as a chance for progress, wisdom and better self-knowledge. Instead of just focusing on the lack of youth or vigor, women can see this as a time to become more self-aware, wise and adventurous.

Conclusion:

Eventually, menopause ends (proving to be a powerful process of change for women everywhere) and becomes more and more some kind of special experience for women – one that they can manage and overcome, armed with self-love as their motto for the trial of the journey of menopause. Womanhood is a lifelong journey where women not only acknowledge but also love, respect and take proper care of their bodies, minds and spirits. Moreover, they survive the turbulence with grace, resilience, and confidence. The self-love you have be your closest companion as you look towards beauty and wisdom in menopause and know that says is a natural stage and a wonderful experience in the whole journey of womanhood.

MENTAL HEALTH

9

EMPOWERING WELLNESS: Understanding Mental Health In Women!!

In today's society, mental health is a critical component of overall wellness, particularly for women who face unique challenges influenced by biological, societal, and psychological factors. This comprehensive guide delves into the prevalence of mental health issues among women, their unique symptoms, and the impact these conditions have on self-love and daily living.

Empowering women through understanding is the first step toward fostering a healthier, more balanced life. Let's discuss this in detail!

Significance of Mental Health in Women

Mental health disorders affect nearly one in five women globally, with conditions like anxiety and depression being more prevalent among women than men. According to the National Institute of Mental Health, the rate of depression among American women is approximately 8.7%, compared to 5.3% among men. Such statistics highlight the pressing need for targeted mental health care and awareness among women.

Mental Health Conditions Specific to Women

Women experience a range of mental health conditions, some of which are influenced by hormonal fluctuations that occur during different life stages. Here, we explore these conditions in detail, highlighting their prevalence, symptoms, and unique challenges for women.

1) Perinatal Depression

Perinatal depression encompasses both prenatal and postpartum depression, affecting women during pregnancy and after childbirth. Studies suggest that approximately 6.5%-20% of women experience some form of perinatal depression. Symptoms can include severe mood swings, anxiety, sadness, and difficulty bonding with the baby. The condition is not just debilitating for the mother but can also affect the well-being and development of the newborn.

2) Premenstrual Dysphoric Disorder (PMDD)

PMDD represents an intense variant of premenstrual syndrome (PMS) and affects approximately 5% of women of childbearing age. Symptoms are more severe than those of PMS and can include extreme mood swings, irritability, depression, and anxiety, which disrupt daily activities and quality of life. These symptoms typically occur during the two weeks leading up to menstruation and subside with the onset of the menstrual period.

3) Perimenopausal Depression

As women transition to menopause, they may experience perimenopausal depression, which affects up to 20% to 40% of women. This form of depression can be triggered by the hormonal fluctuations that occur during this time. Symptoms include mood swings, irritability, anxiety, sadness, and loss of enjoyment in activities previously enjoyed.

4) Eating Disorders

Women are more frequently affected by eating disorders such as nervosa, bulimia nervosa, anorexia and binge eating disorder compared to men. Factors contributing to these disorders in women include societal pressure to maintain a particular body shape, personal and familial stress, and biochemical issues. Eating disorders can have severe health consequences, affecting the cardiovascular, endocrine, and gastrointestinal systems.

5) Anxiety Disorders
Women have a doubled likelihood of experiencing generalized anxiety disorder (GAD), panic disorder, and various other anxiety disorders relative to men. These conditions are characterized by chronic, exaggerated worry and tension that are difficult or seemingly impossible to control. Symptoms include restlessness, fatigue, difficulty concentrating, irritability, muscle tension, and sleep disturbances.

6) Post-Traumatic Stress Disorder (PTSD)
Following a traumatic occurrence, women have a higher propensity to suffer from PTSD, especially when the trauma involves sexual violence. Symptoms of PTSD include flashbacks, severe anxiety, uncontrollable thoughts about the event, and emotional numbness.

Symptoms Of Mental Disorders In Women
Identifying the signs of mental health problems is crucial for enabling women to pursue assistance and take control of their health. Mental health disorders can manifest through a variety of psychological, physical, and behavioral symptoms:

1) Psychological Symptoms:
- **Persistent Sadness or Hopelessness:** A continuous feeling of sadness that affects daily functioning and does not seem to improve.
- **Excessive Worry or Anxiety:** Ongoing, excessive worry that interferes with daily activities and decision-making.

- **Thoughts of Death or Suicide:** Serious symptoms that require immediate intervention, reflecting deep psychological distress.

2) Physical Symptoms:

- **Changes in Sleep Patterns:** Insomnia or oversleeping can significantly impact overall health and energy levels.

- **Appetite or Weight Changes:** Significant fluctuations in weight or eating habits without a clear cause, often linked to depression or anxiety.

- **Fatigue and Pain:** Persistent tiredness and unexplained physical symptoms like headaches or digestive issues are not attributable to other health conditions.

3) Behavioral Symptoms:

- **Substance Misuse:** Increasing reliance on alcohol or drugs as a coping mechanism for mental discomfort or distress.

- **Social Withdrawal:** Pulling away from social interactions and activities that were previously enjoyed can exacerbate feelings of isolation.

- **Irritability or Mood Swings:** Noticeable mood changes that can strain personal and professional relationships.

Impact On Self-Love And Relationships

Mental health issues profoundly affect a woman's self-esteem and her capacity for self-love and healthy relationships. Conditions like depression and anxiety can significantly distort self-perception, impacting how women view their value and worth. This distortion can lead to an erosion of self-esteem, making it difficult for women to advocate for their needs, pursue personal goals, and engage in nurturing relationships.

1) Erosion of Self-Esteem

Women with mental health issues often struggle with feelings of inadequacy and unworthiness. Depression, for instance, can lead individuals to view themselves and their lives in a negative light. Research suggests that women with depression experience some form of self-esteem issues, which can hinder their ability to see themselves accurately and value their own needs.

2) Challenges in Personal Advocacy

Mental health issues may hinder women's ability to assert themselves in both their personal lives and professional environments. According to the Anxiety and Depression Association of America, about 23.4% of American women suffer from anxiety disorders. These conditions often lead to overwhelming fear and worry. As a result, women may avoid situations where they need to advocate for themselves or make important life decisions.

3) Relationship Strain

Mental health issues can also strain relationships, making social connections challenging to maintain. Women with mental health problems might withdraw from friendships and family, reducing their support network when they need it most.

Additionally, the strain can extend to romantic relationships, where emotional volatility or social withdrawal can lead to misunderstandings and conflicts. Studies show that women with depressive disorders are more likely to experience relationship breakdowns, which can further exacerbate feelings of isolation and sadness.

4) Impairment in Pursuing Goals

Depression and anxiety can impair concentration, decision-making, and motivation, all of which are critical in achieving personal and professional goals. These mental health obstacles often hinder numerous women from achieving their goals and aspirations, this often results in a reduced feeling of self-esteem and success.

Seeking Help: Treatment And Support

Effective treatment of mental health conditions involves a comprehensive approach that includes psychotherapy, medication, lifestyle changes, and supportive community networks. Women facing mental health challenges must seek help tailored to their specific physiological and psychological needs. Here's a detailed look at the available treatment options and support mechanisms:

1) Cognitive-behavioral therapy (CBT):

Cognitive Behavioral Therapy (CBT) is an effective approach for addressing several mental health issues, including anxiety and depression. It facilitates individuals in pinpointing and disputing negative cognitive and behavioral patterns, promoting the development of beneficial and constructive ones instead. For women, CBT can be particularly beneficial in addressing the cognitive aspects of conditions like perinatal depression and anxiety by focusing on specific concerns related to women's issues.

2) Antidepressants:

These are commonly prescribed for disorders such as depression and anxiety. Serotonin-norepinephrine reuptake inhibitors (SNRIs) and selective serotonin reuptake inhibitors (SSRIs) are frequently prescribed due to their high efficacy and relatively mild side effects. Medication can be a critical component of treatment, especially when combined with psychotherapy, for achieving the best outcomes.

3) Community Support:

Support groups provide a vital platform for sharing experiences and coping strategies. They help reduce isolation by connecting women with peers undergoing similar challenges. These groups can be incredibly supportive for women dealing with specific issues like eating disorders or postpartum depression, offering a space to share experiences and solutions in a non-judgmental setting.

4) Lifestyle Modifications

Follow these steps to move forward with the strength and resilience to manage her mental health effectively.

- **Regular Exercise:** Physical activity is beneficial in managing symptoms of depression and anxiety. It not only helps in reducing stress but also boosts mood through the release of endorphins.

- **Balanced Diet:** Nutritional psychiatry is becoming increasingly recognized in treating mental health disorders. Consuming a diet abundant in minerals, vitamins, and omega-3 fatty acids can greatly influence both brain function and mood.

- **Adequate Sleep:** Establishing a routine that promotes healthy sleep is crucial, as sleep disturbances can exacerbate symptoms of mental illness.

5) Healthcare Professional Guidance

Starting with a primary healthcare provider is often the best step. They are capable of conducting preliminary evaluations and directing individuals to specialized mental health experts like psychiatrists, psychologists, or clinical social workers, depending on their specific requirements.

Conclusion:

Understanding and addressing mental health in women is not just about treating disorders but also about fostering an environment where self-love and wellness are prioritized. Equipped with appropriate information and support, women can enhance their mental health management, which contributes to a better life quality and more robust relationships.

As society progresses, it becomes increasingly important to support mental health initiatives that empower women to lead fulfilling lives, free from the stigma and constraints of untreated mental health conditions.

KNOW YOUR WORTH: A Guide To Healthy Relationship Standards!!

Romance and relationships can often feel like a treacherous quest for happiness. For women, the journey comes with unique challenges, such as balancing respecting oneself while opening the heart to love.

It's essential to recognize that you deserve a partner who values you, not one who diminishes your worth. This chapter empowers you to set high standards in your relationships, ensuring you never settle for less than you deserve.

Key Standards For Respectful Relationships

Establishing and nurturing meaningful relationships requires a commitment to certain non-negotiable standards. These standards are the foundation of healthy, respectful, and mutually beneficial partnerships. Here, we delve deeper into the key standards every woman should uphold to ensure she is treated with the respect she unequivocally deserves.

1) Refuse to Tolerate Manipulation or Being Played

Never allow anyone to toy with your emotions or treat you as a mere option in their agenda. Relationships founded on mutual respect and comprehension are devoid of manipulation. Remain steadfast in opposing actions that diminish your self-esteem or autonomy.

You deserve a straightforward partner who values your emotions and needs as much as theirs. A partner worth keeping will not need tricks or games to earn your love—they will be consistent in their affection and respect.

2) Reject Dishonesty, Cheating, and Deceit

Trust is not just a fundamental aspect of a relationship; it is essential for survival. Demand transparency and reject any form of deceit. Cheating, whether emotional or physical, is an outright violation of trust and should automatically be a deal-breaker. The wounds caused by betrayal are profound and can enduringly affect your capacity to trust. Commit only to relationships built on trust and honesty from the start.

3) Embracing Traditional Gender Roles in Relationships

In romance, it's vital to maintain traditional views that men should be providers and women the treasured prize. I believe men should display their commitment through acts of provision and chivalry, such as paying for dates and opening doors, emphasizing that women should be treated with the utmost respect and adoration like queens.

These gestures are not just courtesies but fundamental ways a man can show appreciation and respect. This philosophy honors the historical and cultural significance of gender roles, ensuring that women are cherished in relationships and men fulfill their traditional role as providers, fostering a relationship filled with respect and deep affection.

4) Do Not Tolerate Being Used

A relationship should not be one-sided, with one person doing all the giving and the other all the taking. Ensure that your relationship is a partnership of equals, where both parties contribute and receive benefits mutually. This includes sharing responsibilities, supporting each other's ambitions, and being present in need. It may be time to reevaluate the relationship if you feel more like a utility than a partner.

5) Don't Settle for Less Than You Deserve

Recognize your worth, and do not settle for a partner who does not meet your established standards of respect, love, and support. You should know what you desire in a partner—someone who respects you, genuinely loves you, and aligns with your life goals.

Embrace being alone rather than compromising your standards. Use this time to focus on personal growth and preparation for the right person to enter your life. Remember, it is better to be alone and happy than miserable in a relationship.

6) Remember, You Are a Team

In a healthy relationship, remember that you are not fighting each other but are on the same team. Aim to resolve conflicts with understanding and respect, and always strive for solutions that benefit both partners. Effective communication is key: express your needs clearly and listen actively to your partner. This teamwork approach helps strengthen your bond and ensures both partners feel valued and understood.

Understanding Self-Love: Why It Matters

The concept of self-love is not just beneficial; it is essential in the quest for fulfilling relationships. Here's why nurturing self-love is crucial and how it can guide you to healthier relationship choices.

1) Foundation of Self-Esteem

Self-love directly impacts our self-esteem. When you value yourself and understand your worth, you set the standard for how others should treat you. Self-love involves understanding that you merit a relationship in which you are both respected and cherished. It means not settling for less than this standard. If you don't respect yourself, it's difficult to expect or demand that respect from someone else.

2) Decision-making aligned with Self-Respect

With a strong sense of self-love, your decision-making process inherently aligns with your self-respect. You are less likely to tolerate mistreatment or dismiss red flags in a relationship because you recognize that these are not conducive to your well-being. Self-love empowers you to make choices that truly benefit you, supporting your mental, emotional, and physical health.

3) Prioritizing Well-being Over Comfort:

It can be tempting to stay in a relationship simply because it's familiar, even if it's unfulfilling or toxic. Self-love urges you to prioritize your happiness and well-being over the comfort of the known. It encourages you to step out of subpar relationships and into a space where you can be better appreciated. The strength to leave an unsatisfactory relationship comes from self-love and the understanding that your happiness should be a priority.

4) The Role of Self-Care:

Self-love is also about taking care of your own needs through self-care. This includes maintaining your health, nurturing your passions, and ensuring you have time. Self-care reinforces your self-worth and reminds you that your needs are essential. Regular self-care helps you remain at your best, which, in turn, makes you a better partner in any relationship.

Red Flags To Watch For

In pursuing a healthy and fulfilling relationship, it's essential to recognize and respond to red flags early on. These warning signs can signal potential problems undermining the respect, love, and harmony you deserve. Awareness of these red flags protects your heart and empowers you to maintain high standards when choosing a partner. Here's what to watch out for:

- **Lack of Respect:** Disregard for respect is a major warning sign in any relationship. Should your partner regularly undermine your thoughts, diminish your accomplishments, or treat you with disdain, it's evident they don't appreciate you properly. A truly respectful partner will pay attention, rejoice in your successes, and treat you as an equal.

- **Financial Instability and Lack of Ambition:** While love is not measured by wealth, financial instability can strain a relationship, especially if one partner consistently relies on the other for financial support without effort to improve their situation. Similarly, lacking ambition or motivation can signify a lack of responsibility. It's important to have a partner who is financially responsible and motivated to grow both for their own sake and the relationship's health.

- **Multiple Partners and Unresolved Commitments:** Having children with multiple partners without a history of long-term commitment or marriage can be a significant red flag. It may indicate a lack of responsibility and commitment, raising concerns about a person's ability to maintain serious and stable relationships. This pattern might also suggest issues with managing financial and emotional responsibilities across multiple families.

- **Not Treating You as You Deserve:** Everyone deserves to be treated with love and respect. These are significant red flags if you feel consistently undervalued or your partner's actions repeatedly make you feel unworthy or unloved. Your relationship should enhance your self-esteem, not diminish it.

- **Overwhelming Negativity or Pessimism:** A partner who is constantly pessimistic can drain your energy and impact your mental well-being. While everyone experiences tough times, persistent negativity can create a toxic environment in a relationship, stifling growth and happiness.

The Courage To Be Alone: Embracing Solitude For Growth

Being alone rather than in a detrimental relationship showcases profound strength and self-respect. Being alone grants you invaluable space to grow, reflect, and engage fully with your interests without compromise. This solitude is not just a waiting period—it's an active, enriching experience that prepares you for a future relationship where both partners bring equal value.

Step 1: Self-Development During Solitude

Embrace your single time as an opportunity for substantial personal development. Focus on educational pursuits that broaden your knowledge and skills. Emotionally, take the time to understand deeper aspects of your personality and what drives your happiness.

Spiritually, seek practices that bring peace and grounding through meditation, connecting with nature, or other mindfulness practices. Each area contributes to a well-rounded, fulfilled individual ready to engage in a healthy, balanced relationship.

Step 2: Avoiding Desperation

One of the greatest benefits of embracing solitude is avoiding desperation in relationships. Settling for mere companionship out of fear of being alone can lead to unfulfilling relationships that may hinder personal growth. Recognize that holding out for a partner who truly complements and enhances your life is acceptable and beneficial.

Step 3: Preparing for a True Partnership

Being alone is crucial to establishing your expectations and standards for future relationships. Determine what attributes and values are most important to you in a partner, and understand how they align with your life goals. This clarity will help you avoid future partnerships that don't measure up to your standards, ensuring that when you do choose to enter into a relationship, it's with someone truly right for you.

Final Thoughts:

Hold out for a relationship that respects and enhances your life. Remember, it's not just about finding a man. It's about finding the right man. A relationship should be your safe harbor of mutual respect and love, not a storm of doubts and disrespect. You are worth more than substandard treatment; demand and accept nothing less than the best.

A Guide To Identifying And Exiting Abusive Relationships!!

Abusive relationships can manifest in many forms, often cloaked in the guise of love and care. Particularly insidious is abuse that stems from narcissistic behaviors, which can deeply affect one's self-esteem and sense of reality.

This guide explores the nature of abuse, with a focus on dating a narcissist, recognizing the signs of abuse, and planning a safe exit from such relationships. Keep reading to know more!

What is Abuse?

Abuse is an overarching term for behaviors used by one person to gain and maintain control over another. Various types of abuse include physical, emotional, sexual, and psychological, each capable of leaving long-lasting scars. Abuse can occur in any relationship and may be as subtle as it is devastating.

Identifying Different Types of Abuse:

Understanding the various forms of abuse is crucial for recognizing potentially harmful relationships and seeking help. Abuse can manifest in many ways, each damaging in its own right and often leaving profound and long-lasting impacts on the victim. Here are the common types of abuse:

1. Emotional and Psychological Abuse

This type of abuse is among the most subtle and insidious. It involves the manipulation of emotions and eroding a person's self-esteem through tactics such as constant criticism, verbal insults, humiliation, and isolation. Abusers may also use threats, guilt, and shame to control their partners. Victims might experience a loss of self-confidence, anxiety, and depression, feeling worthless and powerless.

2. Physical Abuse

Physical abuse involves any form of violence or physical harm inflicted on the victim. This can range from seemingly minor acts like slapping or shoving to more severe forms of violence, such as hitting, beating, burning, and other aggressive physical acts. Physical abuse is often used as a tool of control and intimidation, creating a constant state of fear in the victim.

3. Financial Abuse

Financial or economic abuse occurs when the abuser takes control of the victim's financial resources, hindering their capacity to support themselves and forcing them to depend on the abuser financially. This can include tactics like withholding money, stealing from the victim, preventing the victim from working or attending school or accumulating large debts on joint accounts without consent.

4. Sexual Abuse

Sexual abuse in relationships involves any non-consensual sexual act or behavior imposed on the victim. This can range from unwanted touching and sexual remarks to sexual coercion and rape. Sexual abuse often is used by abusers to exert power and control over their partners, significantly impacting the victim's mental and emotional health.

Understanding Narcissistic Behavior in Relationships

A narcissist in a relationship exhibits a specific pattern of behaviors that revolve around a deep need for admiration and a lack of empathy for others. Individuals with narcissistic tendencies often engage in a cycle of pulling their partners close and then pushing them away.

It is a manipulative tactic designed to maintain control and keep their partners off balance. So, while dating a narcissist, you must know about that person's behaviors or patterns.

Narcissistic Traits and Behaviors:

Here's how narcissists typically behave in relationships and the warning signs to watch for:

- **Lack of Empathy:** Narcissists struggle to recognize or respond to their partner's needs or feelings. They often disregard others' emotions, which is particularly damaging in intimate relationships where emotional exchange is crucial.
- **Need for Admiration:** Narcissists crave excessive admiration and attention. In relationships, this can manifest as a demand for compliments, a reaction to criticism with rage or coldness, and a tendency to belittle their partner to elevate themselves.
- **Manipulation:** They often manipulate their partners through emotional blackmail (e.g., threatening self-harm to get their way), gaslighting (making their partner doubt their memory or perception of events), and exploiting their partner's vulnerabilities to maintain control.

Warning Signs of Narcissistic Abuse:

Recognizing the distinct patterns of behavior in a narcissist is crucial; now, let's explore the specific warning signs that signify you may be experiencing narcissistic abuse.

- **Love Bombing:** Initially, a narcissist may shower their partner with praise, gifts, and attention, which can feel intoxicating and create a strong emotional bond. This phase shifts dramatically as the relationship progresses.
  - **Gaslighting:** This is a common and damaging tactic where the narcissist denies the victim's experience, often saying things didn't happen when they did or accusing the victim of making things up.
  - **Isolation:** Narcissists often attempt to isolate their partners from friends, family, and other support networks. They might criticize the victim's closest friends or demand excessive time together.
  - **Jekyll and Hyde Behavior:** Narcissists can be charming and affectionate one moment and cold and aggressive the next without clear provocation, which can be confusing and emotionally draining for their partners.
  - **Projecting:** They frequently project their negative behaviors onto their partners. For example, a narcissistic partner might accuse their significant other of cheating when they are the unfaithful one.
  - **Intimidation and Punishment:** Narcissists often use intimidation and punishment tactics, such as shouting, threatening, or physically aggressive behaviors, to control or punish their partners when they do not comply with their wishes.

Statistics on Women Killed from Domestic Violence

Recent global statistics underscore the severe impact of domestic violence, particularly its fatal consequences for women and girls:

- **Global Fatalities:** In 2020, around 47,000 women and girls worldwide were killed by intimate partners or family members, averaging one death every 11 minutes, according to the U.N. Office on Drugs and Crime.
- **Intimate Partner Violence:** More than 5 women or girls are killed every hour by a family member, with 62% of these fatalities caused by current or former intimate partners.
- **Prevalence:** The World Health Organization reports that 1 in 3 (30%) women globally have experienced physical and/or sexual violence by an intimate partner or non-partner in their lifetime.
- **Severe Physical Violence:** In the United States, 1 in 4 women have faced severe physical violence by an intimate partner, including actions like beating, burning, and strangling.
- **Risk Factors:** The presence of a gun in a domestic situation increases the risk of homicide by 500%, significantly heightening the danger.
- **Youth Vulnerability:** Young women, especially those aged 18-24, are the most commonly abused by an intimate partner.
- **Reporting and Support:** Over 20,000 calls are made to domestic violence hotlines in the U.S. each day, reflecting both the prevalence of abuse and the critical role of support services.
- **Legal and Social Challenges:** Intimate partner violence represents 15% of all violent crime, highlighting the need for robust legal responses and societal change.

Know Your Rights and Resources

It's critical to understand that no form of abuse should ever be considered normal or tolerable. Love should foster respect, support, and kindness, not fear and control. If you are experiencing any form of abuse, remember help is available. Contact the National Domestic Violence Hotline at (800) 799-7233, and in emergencies, don't hesitate to dial 911.

How to Plan a Safe Exit from an Abusive Relationship?

Exiting an abusive relationship requires careful preparation to ensure safety and minimize risk. When dealing with a narcissistic partner who may not easily let go, it becomes even more critical to have a strategic plan in place. Here are essential steps to consider for planning a safe exit:

1. Securing Support and Resources

When planning to leave an abusive relationship, the initial step involves gathering support from reliable friends, family, or professionals who are privy to the situation. This support network can offer emotional encouragement and practical help, which are crucial during the transition.

Engaging with local resources like shelters and advocacy groups also provides essential aid, such as legal advice and temporary housing, which are indispensable for safely navigating the departure from an abusive environment.

2. Documenting the Abuse

It is crucial to document every instance of abuse meticulously. This includes keeping a log with dates, times, descriptions, and any available evidence, such as photographs, videos, or digital communications. Such documentation is critical not only for potential legal proceedings, such as custody battles or divorce, but also for securing restraining orders. These records should be stored securely where the abuser cannot access them, ideally in a digital format protected by strong passwords or in a physical location outside the home.

3. Financial Independence

Financial preparation is key to ensuring a successful exit from an abusive relationship. This process starts with establishing financial independence through setting up a personal bank account and discreetly saving money. Collecting and securing important financial and personal documents—such as bank statements, social security cards, and identification documents—is also vital. These steps help secure the financial autonomy necessary for establishing a new phase of life post-separation.

4. Creating a Detailed Safety Plan

The safety plan involves detailed logistics about when and how to leave. This includes deciding on a safe destination, planning the route, and even the mode of transportation to avoid detection. Packing an emergency bag with essentials such as clothes, medications, important documents, and some cash is critical.

This bag should be kept in an easily accessible place to grab it quickly if a rapid departure becomes necessary. Also, setting up an emergency contact list with quick access to friends, legal aid, and local shelters is important for immediate help during and after the escape.

5. Legal and Aftercare Considerations

Once you are in a safe environment, take additional steps to secure your ongoing safety and begin the legal processes that might be necessary. This might include changing your phone number, updating security on social media accounts, and changing locks if the abuser has keys to your property. Consulting with a lawyer specialized in domestic abuse can guide you in obtaining protective orders and dealing with custody and divorce proceedings.

The Path to Healing and Empowerment:

Embracing self-love is crucial in recognizing and responding to the warning signs of abuse. Too often, empty promises of "I will never do it again" are used to excuse harmful behaviors, with apologies used manipulatively to retain control.

It's vital to understand that you are not to blame for the abuse. Standing firm, valuing your self-worth, and loving yourself enough to walk away can empower you to break free from the cycle of abuse and step into a future where you are respected and truly cared for.

10
EMBRACE YOUR BATTLE
Choose your struggle

Everyone wants happiness, a fulfilling career, a loving family, and stable health. However, these desires are universal and somewhat vague. The deeper, more provocative question is: What suffering are you willing to endure to achieve these desires? This chapter explores the significance of choosing your struggles wisely, understanding that true fulfillment often requires overcoming significant challenges.

The Reality of Desires

Human nature drives us toward seeking happiness, love, success, and health—desires that resonate universally. These aspirations are often glorified in media and culture, painting pictures of an ideal life that everyone is expected to strive for. Whether it's a deeply fulfilling relationship, a prosperous career, or optimal physical health, these goals are seen as benchmarks for a successful life.

1. The Effort Behind the Dreams:

However, the glossy surface often belies the tough reality of achieving and maintaining these ideals. The pursuit of such desires isn't just a journey but a battle, requiring more than mere wanting.

- **Relationships:** While a great relationship is a common goal, the emotional investment it requires is substantial. Effective communication, compromise, and the emotional resilience to handle conflicts are essential. It's about more than finding love; it's about nurturing it daily.

- **Career Success:** Professional achievements are highly coveted but come at the cost of long hours, persistent effort, and often, personal sacrifice. The vision of a corner office might be appealing, but getting there might mean navigating through high-pressure environments, tight deadlines, and sometimes, a cutthroat competition that tests your ethical boundaries.

- **Physical Health:** Similarly, optimal health is not just about absence of illness but involves regular exercise, disciplined eating, and mental well-being. The effort to maintain fitness, especially in a world brimming with quick fixes and fast food, involves a daily commitment that many find challenging.

2. The Contrast Between Desire and Reality

The stark contrast between these desires and the realities of achieving them encapsulates the essence of struggle. This section emphasizes that success in any area of life often demands significant sacrifices and efforts that many are unprepared for or unwilling to make. Understanding this disparity is crucial in setting realistic goals and expectations.

The Concept of Struggle

Choosing your struggle involves more than merely selecting what challenges to face; it's about understanding the depth and significance of the sacrifices you're willing to make to achieve your goals. This choice is far more profound than choosing what to enjoy because it fundamentally shapes your efforts and determines your resilience. While anyone can desire happiness and success, only those ready to endure the necessary hardships will likely attain them.

Impact on Life and Identity

The struggles we choose do more than influence our daily activities—they mold our character and define our identity.

Embracing certain challenges and rejecting others reflect our values, aspirations, and limitations. This active selection process helps carve out our unique paths in life, contributing to who we are and how we are perceived by others.

- **Life Shaping:** When you decide to take on a particular struggle, such as pursuing a demanding career, raising a family, or mastering a new skill, you're setting the course of your life trajectory. These decisions dictate your priorities and where you allocate your time, energy, and resources.

- **Identity Forming:** The struggles you choose can also forge aspects of your identity. For example, overcoming significant challenges can establish you as a resilient person, while choosing to tackle social injustices can frame you as an activist. Each choice adds layers to your personal story, making you unique and distinguished.

Why Does It Matters?

Choosing your struggles wisely is crucial because these decisions have long-lasting impacts on your life's fulfillment and satisfaction. The reality is that the path to achieving profound goals is often laden with difficulties. By consciously deciding which difficulties you're prepared to face, you align your life with your deepest values and potential for growth.

The Nature of True Achievement

The common belief that merely desiring success is enough to achieve it is a significant misconception. While strong desires set the direction for our ambitions, they are just the starting point. True achievement demands more than just desire.

It requires substantial effort, resilience in the face of challenges, and a willingness to navigate through adversity. This section debunks the myth that success comes effortlessly. It emphasizes the need for sustained hard work and overcoming obstacles to realize one's goals.

The Realities of Common Goals

Having established that success is not merely a product of desire, let's explore the hidden challenges behind some common goals like career advancement, starting a business, or maintaining a relationship, and uncover what truly lies beneath the surface of achieving these ambitions.

1. Career Advancement:

Achieving a higher position in the workplace often demands more than just proficiency in your job. It involves enduring long hours, demonstrating political savvy, making personal sacrifices, and sometimes even compromising work-life balance.

For women, the climb up the career ladder can come with additional hurdles, such as overcoming gender biases and managing family responsibilities alongside professional ambitions. Recognizing and understanding these challenges is crucial.

It allows for better preparation and strategic planning, empowering women to navigate their career paths more effectively and with a clear vision of the realities they face.

2. Starting a Business:

Entrepreneurship is often portrayed in the media as a direct route to financial independence and personal freedom. However, the reality of starting and maintaining a business is steeped in risk-taking, dealing with uncertainty, financial instability, and a significant workload, especially in the initial stages.

For those considering this path, understanding these challenges is vital. It helps set realistic expectations and equips entrepreneurs to persevere through the difficulties that come with establishing a new venture. By being prepared for these struggles, potential business owners can develop effective strategies to manage stress and overcome setbacks, increasing their chances of success.

3. Maintaining a Relationship:
Sustaining a healthy and fulfilling relationship requires continuous effort, effective communication, mutual respect, and the ability to resolve conflicts constructively. Beyond these well-known challenges, maintaining intimacy and balancing individual growth with the growth of the partnership are less discussed but equally important aspects.

Recognizing the effort required to nurture a relationship is key. It encourages partners to consciously invest in their relationships, which fosters deeper connections and builds resilience against potential strains. This proactive approach to relationship maintenance is essential for cultivating lasting and supportive partnerships.

Transforming Struggles into Triumphs

Overcoming life's challenges is not just about survival but about using these experiences as a foundation for growth and success. This section provides strategies for turning struggles into strengths and offers practical advice on how to embrace and conquer challenges with the right mindset and resilience.

1. Cultivating a Resilient Mindset

The first step in transforming struggles into triumphs is developing a resilient mindset. Resilience allows us to view challenges not as insurmountable obstacles but as opportunities for personal growth and learning. Here are practical ways to cultivate such a mindset:

- **Reframe Challenges:** Learn to view difficulties as necessary steps towards reaching your goals, rather than setbacks. This reframe can change your emotional response to challenges and increase your determination to overcome them.

- **Embrace Failure as a Teacher:** Accept that failure is a part of the growth process. Analyze your failures to understand what went wrong and how you can improve, turning these lessons into stepping stones towards success.

- **Set Realistic Expectations:** Understand that progress is often incremental and comes with ups and downs. Setting realistic goals and expectations can prevent feelings of discouragement during tough times.

2. Building Emotional Resilience

Emotional resilience is crucial for managing stress and bouncing back from setbacks. Strengthening this aspect involves:

- **Practice Self-Compassion:** Be kind to yourself during tough times. Recognize that struggling does not reflect your worth or capabilities.

- **Develop Coping Strategies:** Identify what helps you relieve stress and keep a positive outlook. This could be activities like yoga, meditation, reading, or spending time in nature.

- **Seek Support:** Don't hesitate to lean on friends, family, or professional counselors when the going gets tough. Sharing your struggles can lighten your emotional load and provide new perspectives.

3. Leveraging Challenges for Growth

Turning struggles into triumphs also means using your experiences to foster personal and professional growth:

- **Identify Growth Opportunities:** Each challenge holds a lesson. After facing a difficulty, take time to reflect on what you've learned and how this knowledge can be applied in the future.

- **Expand Your Skill Set:** Challenges often force us to develop new skills or hone existing ones. Embrace this as an opportunity to become more versatile and capable.

- **Maintain a Long-Term Perspective:** Keep your eyes on your long-term goals. Remind yourself that current struggles are just part of the journey towards those goals.

Final Thoughts:

We recognized that true fulfillment and achievement are not the products of mere desire, but the result of confronting and mastering the inevitable struggles life presents. Whether advancing in one's career, nurturing a relationship, or launching a business, each requires a blend of resilience, strategic planning, and emotional fortitude.

This chapter has armed you with insights and strategies to transform these challenges into triumphs, emphasizing that the most rewarding successes are those hard-won through perseverance and growth. As you move forward, let each struggle shape you into a more robust and capable version of yourself, fully equipped to achieve your most cherished goals.

THE STRUGGLE FOR WHOLENESS: EMPOWERING WOMEN TO BREAK CYCLES AND CULTIVATE SELF-LOVE

Introduction

In a world that often diminishes the struggles and experiences of women, it is crucial to address the patterns and cycles that can hinder personal growth and fulfillment. Too often, women find themselves repeating the same mistakes, choosing partners who do not align with their values or treat them with respect. The consequences of these choices can be devastating, leading to a lifetime of heartbreak, insecurity, and unfulfilled potential.

This piece aims to shed light on the importance of self-accountability, healing, and personal growth for women. It is a call to action, a rallying cry for women to break free from the shackles of toxic relationships, unhealthy patterns, and societal pressures. By embracing self-love, seeking support, and cultivating a deep understanding of one's worth, women can reclaim their power and build the foundations for healthy, fulfilling relationships with themselves and others.

The Cycle of Unhealthy Relationships

"We accept the love we think we deserve." – Stephen Chbosky

All too often, women find themselves trapped in a cycle of unhealthy relationships, repeatedly choosing partners who exhibit the same toxic behaviors or fail to meet their needs. This pattern is often rooted in deep-seated insecurities, past traumas, or a lack of self-worth. When a woman has not fully addressed her emotional wounds or unresolved issues, she may unconsciously gravitate toward familiar patterns, even if they are detrimental to her well-being.

The consequences of this cycle can be devastating. Women may find themselves in abusive relationships, enduring emotional, physical, or psychological harm. They may compromise their values, settle for partners who are unfaithful, or accept disrespectful treatment. In some cases, women may even find themselves with multiple children from different partners, a situation that can be challenging and emotionally taxing.

It is important to recognize that this cycle is not a reflection of a woman's worth or character. Rather, it is a symptom of deeper issues that require attention and healing. By acknowledging the patterns and taking responsibility for breaking them, women can begin the journey toward self-empowerment and healthy relationships.

The Importance of Healing and Self-Love

"Self-love is not selfish; it is a necessary step towards loving others." – Bell hooks

To break the cycle of unhealthy relationships, women must first prioritize their own healing and self-love. This process involves acknowledging and addressing past traumas, insecurities, and emotional wounds. It means seeking support from therapists, counselors, or support groups to work through these issues in a safe and nurturing environment.

Healing is not a linear process, but a journey of self-discovery and self-acceptance. It requires vulnerability, courage, and a willingness to confront painful experiences and emotions. However, the rewards of this journey are immeasurable – a deeper sense of self-worth, resilience, and the ability to form healthy, fulfilling relationships.

Self-love is a critical component of this healing process. It involves cultivating an unconditional acceptance and appreciation for oneself, flaws and all. It means recognizing one's inherent worth and value, independent of external validation or societal expectations. When a woman truly loves and values herself, she is less likely to settle for partners or situations that diminish her worth or compromise her boundaries.

Setting Boundaries and Establishing Standards

"The boundaries you set for others are a reflection of the boundaries you set for yourself." – Brené Brown

As women embark on their journey of healing and self-love, it becomes essential to establish healthy boundaries and standards for the relationships they choose to engage in. This involves developing a deep understanding of one's values, needs, and non-negotiables in a partner.

Before entering into a new relationship, it is crucial for women to take the time to reflect on their past experiences, identify patterns or red flags, and establish clear criteria for what they will and will not accept in a partner. This process may involve asking probing questions about a potential partner's character, values, goals, and treatment of others.

Some key areas to explore include:
1. **Emotional Maturity:** How does the individual handle conflicts, communicate their needs, and navigate challenging situations? Do they exhibit emotional

intelligence and a willingness to work through issues in a healthy manner?
2. **Financial Stability and Responsibility:** Does the individual have a steady income, manage their finances responsibly, and demonstrate the ability to support themselves and potential dependents? Are they committed to contributing their fair share in a partnership?
3. **Respect and Commitment:** How does the individual treat others, especially those closest to them? Do they exhibit respect, loyalty, and a commitment to personal growth and the growth of the relationship?
4. **Personal Values and Goals:** Are the individual's values and life goals aligned with your own? Do they share a similar vision for the future, and are they willing to work together to achieve shared goals?
5. **Accountability and Integrity:** Does the individual take responsibility for their actions and hold themselves accountable? Do they exhibit honesty, integrity, and a willingness to grow and improve themselves?
6. By establishing clear standards and boundaries, women can empower themselves to make informed decisions about potential partners and avoid repeating past mistakes. It is a powerful act of self-love and a declaration of one's worth and value.

Cultivating Healthy Mindsets and Habits

"The mind is everything. What you think, you become." – Buddha

Breaking cycles and cultivating self-love also involves adopting healthy mindsets and habits that support personal growth and well-being. This process requires conscious effort and a commitment to ongoing self-improvement.

One crucial aspect of this journey is learning to be comfortable with solitude and independence. Too often, women rush from one relationship to the next, seeking external validation or a sense of completion from a partner. However, true fulfillment and happiness must come from within. By embracing the power of solitude, women can learn to find joy and contentment in their own company, cultivate self-awareness, and develop a deep appreciation for their unique strengths and qualities.

Another important mindset shift involves reframing the concept of relationships and romantic partnerships. Rather than viewing a partner as a means to "complete" oneself or fill a void, women should strive to approach relationships as a union of two whole, self-sufficient individuals who choose to share their lives and grow together

This mindset shift can be accompanied by practical habits that foster self-love and personal growth, such as:

1. Engaging in self-care practices: This can include activities like journaling, meditation, exercise, or pursuing creative hobbies that bring joy and fulfillment.

2. Building a supportive community: Surrounding oneself with positive, uplifting individuals who encourage personal growth and celebrate one's journey can be invaluable.

3. Continuous learning and personal development: Committing to ongoing education, whether through formal classes, workshops, or self-study, can help women expand their knowledge, skills, and perspectives.

4. Setting and pursuing personal goals: Establishing clear, achievable goals in various areas of life (career, health, relationships, etc.) can provide a sense of purpose and direction.

By cultivating healthy mindsets and habits, women can build a strong foundation of self-love and personal fulfillment, which will ultimately attract healthier, more aligned relationships into their lives.

The Power of Walking Away

"The most powerful thing a woman can do is walk away." – Unknown

In the pursuit of healthy relationships and personal growth, women must also learn the power of walking away from situations or individuals that no longer serve their best interests. This act of self-preservation is a testament to one's self-love and a refusal to settle for anything less than what they truly deserve.

Walking away can be a challenging and emotionally fraught decision, especially if a woman has invested significant time, effort, or emotional energy into a relationship. However, it is important to recognize when a partnership has become toxic, stagnant, or incompatible with one's values and aspirations.

Signs that it may be time to walk away include:

- Consistent disrespect or diminishment of one's worth
- Emotional, physical, or psychological abuse
- Infidelity or a pattern of dishonesty
- Incompatible life goals or values
- Lack of emotional availability or commitment
- Unresolved issues or an unwillingness to seek help or grow together

While the decision to walk away can be difficult, it is a powerful act of self-love and a declaration of one's boundaries and standards.

By choosing to remove oneself from unhealthy or unfulfilling situations, women create space for new opportunities, personal growth, and the potential for healthier, more aligned relationships to enter their lives.

Conclusion

The journey towards self-love, healing, and healthy relationships is a lifelong endeavor that requires courage, vulnerability, and a deep commitment to personal growth. It is a path fraught with challenges and obstacles, but one that ultimately leads to a sense of empowerment, fulfillment, and a deeper connection with oneself and others.

By breaking cycles of unhealthy relationships, seeking support and healing, establishing clear boundaries and standards.

11

A WOMAN'S GUIDE TO FEARLESS INDEPENDENCE AMBITION

Fear is a natural emotion but can also be a formidable barrier, especially for women facing pivotal life changes or challenging societal norms. This chapter is not just about understanding fear, but about using it as a stepping stone to inspire and empower you. It's about conquering your fears, carving your path to success, and claiming your independence and ambitions. Dive into these pages ready to shed the doubts that have held you back and embrace the strength that defines you.

Understanding Fear And Its Impacts

It's crucial to recognize that fear, as we know it, is an emotional response triggered by perceived threats, whether real or imagined. It's a fundamental survival mechanism that, when it becomes constant or irrational, can hinder personal and professional growth. This understanding is the key to managing and overcoming fear.

Women, particularly those facing significant life decisions or undergoing transitions such as career changes, relationship evolutions, or personal development milestones, often experience unique manifestations of fear. These are not just abstract concepts, but fears that you may have felt too-fear of failure, fear of success, fear of judgment, or even fear of not fulfilling expected roles.

Psychological Impact of Fear:

The psychological impact of fear is deep, often preventing women from reaching their full potential by confining them to their comfort zones. Fear distorts perception, amplifying potential failures and downplaying success opportunities, leading to anxiety and a decline in self-confidence and influence. This can keep women stuck in unfulfilling situations and limit their growth.

Unchecked fear also hampers women's contributions to leadership and teamwork, as it may deter them from voicing opinions or accepting new challenges. In personal life, it can cause dependency and loss of individuality, holding women back from expressing their true needs and desires.

The Role Of Self-Belief In Overcoming Fear

Self-confidence is a pivotal force in overcoming fear. The internal power pushes you to take action despite uncertainties and potential setbacks. For women especially, building self-confidence is essential for breaking the cycle of fear that hinders progress toward personal and professional goals.

Strategies to Build Self-Belief:

To cultivate self-belief and adopt a fearless approach to life, consider these effective strategies:

- **Positive Affirmations:** Start each day with positive affirmations such as "I am capable," "I am worthy of success," and "I am strong." These phrases can significantly alter your mindset by transforming negative self-talk into a positive belief system. Regularly remind yourself of your strengths to build a robust foundation of self-confidence.
- **Setting Small, Achievable Goals:** Fear often arises from daunting tasks. Break your larger goals into smaller, manageable steps. This approach makes challenges less intimidating and allows you to celebrate minor victories, each of which reinforces your confidence and helps overcome fear.
- **Celebrating Personal Successes:** Regularly celebrate your achievements, big or small. Recognizing and rewarding yourself reinforces positive emotions and builds momentum.

Simple acts of celebration, like reflecting on accomplishments or sharing them with loved ones, remind you of your capabilities and motivate you to continue progressing.

Empowering Actions Toward Dreams:

Women must believe in themselves, which often involves shifting the focus from fear-driven inaction to possibility-driven actions. Whether it's returning to school, launching a new business, or pursuing a long-held dream, the journey starts with believing that success is attainable. With each step forward, powered by enhanced self-belief, fear becomes less of a blockade and more of a motivator to push boundaries.

Remember, self-confidence doesn't appear overnight. It's built through consistent practice and embracing challenges as opportunities to grow. By applying these strategies, you empower yourself to move beyond fear, making room for endless possibilities where your dreams can thrive.

Identity And Independence In Relationships

In many relationships, it's common for women to lose a sense of their identity, finding themselves defined more by their partnership than by their qualities or achievements. While often happening subtly, this merging of identities can diminish personal growth and independence, leading to a loss of self.

Cultivating Personal Goals and Dreams:

Having personal goals and dreams is vital, not just for your sense of self but also for your overall well-being. These aspirations should be nurtured regardless of your relationship status. They remind you of your capabilities and passions, which are independent of your role as a partner.

Whether pursuing a career ambition, engaging in creative projects, or traveling solo, these activities help fortify your identity and ensure that the relationship never overshadows your sense of self.

How to preserve Independence?

As you nurture your personal goals and engage in activities that reflect your unique interests, it's equally important to establish practical strategies that help maintain your independence within a relationship. Here are some effective ways to ensure you continue to thrive as an individual:

- **Set Personal Goals:** Define what you want to achieve outside your relationship. These can be career-oriented, educational, or personal development goals. Write them down and review them regularly to keep your ambitions clear and focused.
- **Engage in Individual Activities:** Make time for activities you love or want to explore independently. This could include taking classes, starting new hobbies, or going out with friends. Each partner needs to have their own space and freedom to grow.
- **Communicate Openly:** Discuss the importance of personal space and independence with your partner. Clear communication about your needs and boundaries is vital for maintaining a healthy balance between togetherness and individuality.
- **Support Each Other's Goals:** Encourage and support your partner's ambitions. A healthy relationship thrives when both partners are individually fulfilled, and celebrating each

other's successes can strengthen the bond and mutual respect.

Financial Independence As Freedom

Being financially independent means you don't have to rely on anyone else for your financial needs. This independence is liberating, especially for women who may face unexpected turns in their personal lives, such as a divorce or a partner's sudden illness. It ensures that you are never trapped in a relationship or situation due to financial constraints and allows you to make the best decisions for your personal and emotional well-being.

Practical Steps Toward Financial Freedom

Now that you know the importance of financial independence, let's explore practical steps you can take to secure your financial freedom. Here's how to lay the foundation for a financially independent future:

1. Develop Marketable Skills

It's vital to have skills that can be quickly leveraged in the workforce, especially for stay-at-home moms. Whether it's freelance writing, graphic design, virtual assistance, or another field with flexible work options, having a skill set that allows you to earn income independently is crucial. Consider online courses or local workshops to help you gain or improve these skills.

2. Smart Financial Planning

Start by creating a budget to track your income and expenses. Understand where your money goes each month, and identify areas where you can cut back. Use budgeting apps or tools to streamline this process and make it a regular monthly routine.

3. Saving for the Future

Building a savings buffer is critical. Aim to save at least three to six months' expenses for emergencies. Open a savings account that yields interest and make it a habit to deposit a small portion of your income regularly, no matter how small.

4. Investing Wisely

Investing is a powerful way to grow wealth over time. Educate yourself on investing in stocks, bonds, mutual funds, or real estate. Consider consulting a financial advisor to tailor an investment strategy that fits your risk tolerance and financial goals.

5. Protect Your Assets

Understand the importance of having insurance and an updated will. These are crucial to a sound financial plan, protecting your assets and your family's future.

Breaking Out Of Comfort Zones

Staying within a comfort zone offers a sense of safety and familiarity, which is why many women hesitate to step beyond its boundaries. However, the comfort zone is also a barrier to growth and achievement. Breaking free from it boosts personal and professional development and empowers women to pursue their dreams and goals without fear.

Why do Women Stay in their Comfort Zones?

Many women remain in their comfort zones due to fear of the unknown, fear of failure, or even fear of success. These fears are often magnified by self-doubt and the imposter syndrome, where women might feel they are not good enough to achieve higher goals or take on more challenging roles. The comfort zone feels safe but is limiting and can prevent women from reaching their full potential.

Benefits of Stepping Out:

Stepping out of your comfort zone is where growth happens. It exposes you to new challenges and opportunities, enhancing your skills and confidence. It can lead to better job positions, the successful launch of a new business, or the pursuit of a long-desired personal goal. Moving beyond comfort zones also fosters resilience, teaching you to adapt and thrive in various situations.

Embrace Higher Aspirations:

Remember, every successful woman was once a beginner who dared to step out of her comfort zone. The path to achieving your dreams is paved with challenges, but each is an opportunity to grow stronger and become more confident. Embrace the discomfort; it is a sign of progress and a precursor to success. Your dreams and goals are worth the effort and the risk. You can reach new heights and fulfill your potential with persistence and resilience.

Why Risk-Taking is Essential?

Risk-taking pushes you beyond the familiar and the comfortable, leading to new experiences that can reshape your understanding of what is possible. Whether you're changing careers, starting a new business, or making a significant personal change, each risk represents a chance to significantly alter your life's trajectory.

Taking risks also serves as a powerful antidote to fear. It forces you to confront potential failures head-on, turning them from vague threats into manageable challenges. This can diminish the fear associated with the unknown and boost your confidence and resilience.

Strategic Risk-Taking:

While the idea of taking risks might sound daunting, it can be approached in a measured and strategic manner:

- **Assess the Risks:** Not all risks are created equal. Evaluate the potential outcomes of the risk you're considering. What are the possible benefits? What are the downsides? Understanding these can help you make informed decisions.
- **Start Small:** If taking a big risk is too intimidating, start with smaller risks with manageable consequences. This could be as simple as pitching a new idea at work, joining a class, or going on a solo travel adventure.
- **Prepare for Outcomes:** Once you decide to take a risk, prepare for the possible outcomes. For example, if you're starting a business, have a financial buffer in place. If you're changing careers, develop the skills necessary for your new path in advance.
- Learn from Failure: View failures not as setbacks but as learning opportunities. Each risk taken is a lesson learned, helping you build a richer, more experienced perspective on life.
- **Celebrate Wins:** When risks pay off, take the time to celebrate. Acknowledging and reveling in these successes can reinforce the value of stepping out of your comfort zone and encourage you to continue taking risks in the future.

Building A Support Network

Your support network serves multiple roles: cheerleaders, including friends, family, mentors, and professional networks, encourage you during challenging times; advisors provide guidance; and connectors open doors to new opportunities. These relationships can lift you when you doubt yourself and provide crucial insights and resources when you need them the most.

Empowerment Through Your Network:

A well-cultivated support network empowers you by enhancing your confidence and ability to act despite challenges. It can transform a daunting journey into an achievable one, with the collective strength of your supporters propelling you forward.

Remember, the right support at the right time can be a game-changer in your personal and professional life. By building and maintaining your network, you ensure you have a powerful ally in your corner, ready to help you succeed in all your endeavors.

Closing Notes:

Fear should not define your limits. You can achieve remarkable independence and ambition by understanding and managing your fears, maintaining independence, and leveraging support systems. Remember, overcoming fear and achieving your dreams does not happen overnight; it is a persistent path of self-discovery, courage, and resilience.

Empower yourself today by taking the first step out of your comfort zone and pushing forward. Your potential is limitless, and your journey to fearless independence and ambition is beginning.

Embrace Your Radiance: A Journey to Self-Love

As we turn the final page of this journey together, remember that every chapter in your life begins with you. You hold the pen that can script a narrative of self-love and triumph. You are beautiful - not just in the reflection of the mirror but in the strength of your spirit and the resilience of your heart. You've faced your fears, confronted your challenges, and embarked on the courageous path of self-discovery and self-love. And now, as you stand on the abyss of a new beginning, I want you to know just how beautiful and radiant you truly are.

Facing your fears and embracing your challenges is not just an act of courage; it is an act of profound love for yourself. Each step you take, no matter how small, is a step toward realizing your worth and potential. You are a masterpiece - a symphony of strength, resilience, and boundless potential. With each step you've taken on this journey, you've uncovered hidden treasures within yourself - gems of wisdom, compassion, and unwavering love. And as you continue to embrace your truth and honor your worth, these treasures will continue to shine brightly, illuminating the path ahead with hope, joy, and endless possibilities.

As we navigate the path of self-discovery and personal growth, let's not forget to pursue our dreams with unwavering determination and passion. Our dreams are the manifestations of our deepest desires and aspirations, and they deserve to be pursued with wholehearted dedication. Whether it's starting a business, traveling the world, or exploring a creative passion, let's believe in ourselves and take bold steps towards making our dreams a reality.

Let today be the day you commit to seeing yourself with the same awe and wonder that the world does. Start by whispering to yourself in the quiet moments, 'I am worthy. I am beautiful. I am enough. 'Let these words be your anchor in times of doubt and your wings in times of joy.

Remember the journey of self-love is not a race. It is a lifelong exploration that ebbs and flows like the ocean. You may face storms and calm alike, but each wave brings you closer to the shores of your own heart. Ladies, hear this: You are worthy more than you can ever imagine. Within the depths of your being lies an indomitable spirit - a reservoir of strength, resilience, and untapped potential waiting to be unleashed. You are not just capable of greatness; you are destined for it. But first, you must believe it with every fiber of your being.

Carry forward the lessons of kindness, courage, and resilience you've gathered along the way. Let them light your path as you continue to grow, explore, and love yourself more deeply every day.

As you close this book, open your heart to the endless possibilities that await. Stand tall, dream boldly, and love yourself fiercely. For in loving yourself, you embrace the very essence of life itself. You are not just surviving; you are thriving. You are not just living; you are blooming in the fullness of your own unique beauty.

Go forth with the knowledge that you are supported, cherished, and admired - not just for the person you will become but for the magnificent person you are right now. Remember, in the garden of life, you are the most exquisite flower.

In the gentle closing of our shared journey through this book, it's crucial that we turn our attention to a cornerstone of self-love and personal growth: our health. Not just the health of our minds and hearts, but the vital, often overlooked health of our bodies. True self-love encompasses a respect and care for our physical selves, understanding that our mental aspirations and spiritual peace are deeply interconnected with our bodily well-being.

Embrace the full spectrum of health. It's essential to follow your dreams and chase your passions, but equally important to nurture the vessel that carries you through every step of that journey - your body. Regular checkups with your doctor are not just procedural; they are profound acts of self-respect. They are your personal declaration that you value the life you lead and the dreams you chase. Yearly mammograms, screenings, and the advice of professionals are foundations upon which you build a life of vibrant, active engagement.

It's entirely okay, and indeed brave, to acknowledge when you might need support beyond the physical. Seeing a therapist or psychologist is not a sign of weakness but of strength. It is a clear signal that you are taking charge, prioritizing your well-being, and choosing to thrive not just survive.

I have witnessed the shock and sorrow of losing friends unexpectedly in their prime, vibrant years of their fifties. It's a poignant reminder that life is precious, and often fragile. Pay close attention to your body's signals. Do not dismiss the small, quiet whispers that something might not be right. These whispers, if listened to, can be lifesaving. Whether it's an unexplained pain, a lingering fatigue, or emotional lows that don't seem to lift, responding to these signs by seeking a health provider is a critical step in honoring and preserving your life.

So, as you step forward from this page into the rest of your life, carry with you a commitment to your health. Let it be as deep and passionate as your commitment to your dreams. Your health is your strength, your foundation, your lifeline. Treasure it, nurture it, and watch as it amplifies every other beautiful aspect of your life. Live fully, love deeply, and nourish the body that allows you to do so. This is not just self-love; this is self-reverence.

In this journey toward self-love and holistic well-being, there is a profound strength found not only in nurturing ourselves but in extending that care to others, especially among women. Our ability to flourish is immensely enhanced when we support each other. Unfortunately, judgment and jealousy have too often shadowed the path we walk together. These emotions not only hinder our own growth but also fracture the bonds that could become our greatest sources of strength and encouragement.

`Remember, true security in oneself leaves no room for insecurity about others. When you feel whole and valued on your own, you are more likely to view another's success not as a threat but as an inspiration. It is vital to cultivate a community where we can genuinely rejoice in each other's wins and support each other through losses. Such a community thrives on empathy and compassion, recognizing that while today might be her winning season, tomorrow could be yours. Every victory for one woman can lift all who surround her.

The Bible wisely advises, "Give, and it shall be given unto you." This timeless principle holds especially true in the fabric of female relationships. What you sow in support and kindness, you will likely reap in abundance. It is crucial to resist the pull of jealousy and bitterness. Such emotions are thieves that rob us not only of potential joy but of actual opportunities. By holding back your support or harboring ill will, you aren't safeguarding your worth; you're stunting your growth and that of others.

Therefore, start networking with other women, not with the sole intention of gaining for yourself, but to build a network of mutual support and shared growth. Be the woman who applauds someone else's accomplishments, who lends a hand when others falter. Be there for women in need, offer a word of encouragement, a gesture of kindness. You can't be upset at another woman for pursuing her dreams, especially if you haven't taken that step yourself. The energy you invest in being supportive rather than envious multiplies and comes back to enrich your life.

So, let us strive to be less judgmental and more generous in our judgments. Let's transform envy into admiration, competition into camaraderie. As we foster this new culture of support and mutual respect, we not only enhance our own lives but also forge a legacy of empowerment for all the women who follow. This is not merely about being nice - it's about being wise, about being strong, and about being true not only to others but to the very essence of our collective potential.

To stride confidently into the world, embracing every facet of your being, is perhaps the greatest gift you can give yourself. Confidence is not merely feeling good about how you look or what you achieve - it is a profound, unshakeable belief in your own worth. It involves understanding your intrinsic value, recognizing your strengths, and accepting your flaws with grace.

Having high self-esteem is essential; it acts as the backbone of your endeavors and interactions. When you love and value yourself, you naturally set a higher standard for how you expect to be treated by others. This self-respect becomes a beacon, guiding others on how to engage with you. It fosters relationships rooted in mutual respect and genuine support.

Embracing self-love is indeed a transformative journey. It is about acknowledging that you are worthy of your own care, affection, and respect. It's about stopping the critical internal voice that focuses only on flaws and starting to celebrate your uniqueness, your talents, and even your imperfections. These are not detractions from your value but aspects that make you distinctively you.

12 DEALING WITH PAIN

EMBRACING YOUR BODY

INTRODUCTION:

In society, where unrealistic beauty standards are omnipresent, women often find themselves grappling with feelings of inadequacy regarding their bodyweight. Yet, what if we dared to shift our perspective?

What if we wholeheartedly embraced our bodies, acknowledging that our size holds no sway over our inherent worth? Within the pages ahead, we embark on a transformative journey of self-discovery and empowerment. Here, we delve deep into the profound notion that women can not only love their size but also cultivate unwavering confidence from within. By nurturing a foundation of self-love and embracing the unique beauty of our bodies, we unlock boundless potential to flourish in every facet of our lives.

It's a journey that transcends physical appearance, empowering us to embrace our authenticity and reclaim our narrative with grace and resilience. So let us embark on this voyage together, as we celebrate the beauty of every shape and size, knowing that true empowerment stems from embracing ourselves, unapologetically.

THE POWER OF SELF-LOVE:

At the core of embracing our bodyweight lies the transformative power of self-love. It's the profound act of accepting and appreciating ourselves in entirety, embracing our flaws alongside our strengths, that ignites a radiant aura of confidence and inner fortitude. Self-love transcends the confines of achieving a specific size or weight; instead, it's a journey of embracing our individuality and reveling in the remarkable capabilities of our bodies.

Through the practice of self-love, we lay down a sturdy foundation of confidence, empowering ourselves to pursue our aspirations and ambitions with unyielding determination. It's this deep reservoir of self-assurance that propels us forward, enabling us to confront challenges head-on and seize opportunities with unwavering conviction.

With self-love as our guiding light, we embark on a journey of empowerment, fully embracing our worth and potential, and embracing the beauty of our bodies in all their uniqueness and magnificence.

OVERCOMING INSECURITIES:

It's an unfortunate reality that many women grapple with insecurities and diminished self-esteem, deeply influenced by the relentless societal pressures surrounding body image. However, what if we dared to view these insecurities through a different lens? What if we saw them not as burdens, but as catalysts for growth and self-discovery? By bravely acknowledging our insecurities and committing to actively overcoming them, we reclaim agency over our own narrative, infusing it with a profound sense of self-compassion and empowerment.

Whether through embarking on a journey of physical wellness through exercise and diet, or through nurturing our mental and emotional well-being with various forms of self-care, we hold within us the transformative power to transmute our insecurities into wellsprings of resilience and strength. It's through this courageous act of self-reflection and self-improvement that we pave the way for a future where our insecurities no longer hold dominion over us but instead serve as stepping stones toward our most empowered selves.

BUILDING CONFIDENCE:

Confidence isn't an innate trait bestowed upon us at birth; rather, it's a quality we nurture through diligent self-care and unwavering self-compassion. By conscientiously prioritizing our physical and emotional well-being, we lay the groundwork for cultivating the unwavering confidence essential for navigating life's myriad challenges with grace and resilience. Whether we embark on a journey of regular exercise to invigorate our bodies, nourish ourselves with wholesome foods to sustain our vitality, or engage in mindfulness practices and introspective self-reflection to foster inner peace, each proactive step serves as a potent catalyst in fortifying our confidence and embracing ourselves unconditionally. It's through these deliberate acts of self-investment and self-love that we empower ourselves to embrace our true essence and celebrate our inherent worth, exactly as we are. In nurturing our confidence, we not only honor our authentic selves but also equip ourselves with the resilience needed to thrive amidst life's ebbs and flows.

The journey of women embracing their bodyweight is a profound journey of self-discovery, empowerment, and, ultimately, self-love. It's a journey that transcends the superficial confines of societal norms and beauty standards, inviting women to embark on a deeply personal exploration of their own worth and inherent beauty. By daring to challenge the notion that size dictates our value, we liberate ourselves from the shackles of comparison and self-doubt, paving the way for a transformative shift in perspective.

In this journey, we arm ourselves with the tools of self-compassion and resilience, determined to overcome the insecurities that once held us captive. Through acts of self-care, whether it be through nourishing our bodies with wholesome foods, engaging in regular exercise, or prioritizing our mental and emotional well-being through mindfulness and self-reflection, we cultivate the unwavering confidence needed to navigate life's twists and turns with grace and fortitude.

Let us embrace our bodies with boundless love and gratitude, honoring the intricate tapestry of our physical forms and celebrating the unique beauty that each of us possesses. For true beauty, we discover, emanates from the depths of our souls, radiating outward in waves of authenticity and self-assurance.

Together, let us endeavor to create a world where every woman feels emboldened to embrace her true self, where confidence reigns supreme, and where love knows no bounds. In this world, size holds no sway over our worth, for we recognize that our value lies not in our appearance, but in the richness of our character and the depth of our hearts.

With unwavering determination and solidarity, let us forge ahead, championing a vision of inclusivity, acceptance, and self-love for women of every shape and size. For it is in this collective journey of empowerment that we find the true essence of our humanity and the boundless potential that lies within each and every one of us.

Forged in Fire: The Phoenix Rising

Introduction

One of life's certainties is going through pain at one point. Pain is an inevitable feeling intertwined with our experiences. Through pain, we get to have the most profound lessons and opportunities for growth. Life isn't a fairytale. We all experience pain, heartbreak, and loss. It's a universal truth of the human experience. For many women, this pain hits hard. A brutal divorce, the loss of a mother, the unimaginable grief of losing a child. These experiences leave scars and a deep ache that can feel overwhelming. But within that pain lies an incredible power, a strength waiting to be unleashed.

This article isn't about minimizing your pain. It's about acknowledging its presence while offering a glimpse of possibility. The fire of hardship can forge you into something remarkable – a woman of resilience, compassion, and unwavering strength.

Understanding Pain:

Sarah had always been the pillar of strength for her family, holding back tears and putting on a brave face even in the most challenging times. However, when she faced the sudden loss of her mother, Sarah found herself crumbling under the weight of grief. It was only when she allowed herself to embrace vulnerability and share her pain with loved ones that she began to find healing. Through tearful conversations and heartfelt embraces, Sarah discovered that true strength lies not in hiding her pain but in embracing it with courage and authenticity.

Pain is a universal language spoken in whispers of heartbreak, loss, and betrayal. It transcends barriers of gender, age, and culture, leaving an indelible mark on the human soul. For many women, the journey through pain takes various forms, from the shattered dreams of divorce to the unbearable grief of losing a child or a mother. Yet, within the depths of this anguish lies the potential for profound transformation and empowerment. The first step to transformation is acknowledging the pain. Ignoring it only allows it to fester. Let yourself feel the sting of loss, the hollowness of heartbreak. Cry. Scream into a pillow. Write in a journal until the ink runs dry. Permit yourself to feel the full force of your emotions, the crushing grief, the searing anger, and the paralyzing fear. Bottling it up will only hinder your healing.

The Phoenix Rising - Transforming Your Pain

Mia's divorce left her feeling adrift and lost, questioning the purpose behind her pain. As she navigated the turbulent waters of separation, Mia turned to journaling as a means of processing her emotions and finding clarity amidst the chaos. Through writing, she uncovered hidden insights and revelations about herself and her relationship, gaining a newfound sense of empowerment and self-awareness. In the depths of her despair, Mia discovered that even amidst the wreckage of her marriage, there were seeds of growth waiting to be cultivated.

Pain can be a destructive force, or it can be the catalyst for incredible transformation. When channeled effectively, it becomes your fuel, propelling you forward. While pain may initially feel like an insurmountable obstacle, it also presents an opportunity for introspection and growth. Through the process of introspection, we can uncover valuable lessons and insights that deepen our understanding of ourselves and the world around us. By reframing our perspective and searching for meaning amidst adversity, we can transcend our pain and emerge as more resilient individuals.

Ask yourself:

- What lessons did this experience teach me about myself and the world?
- What hidden strengths did I discover within myself during this time?
- How can I use this experience to help others who might be facing similar struggles?

Cultivating the Art of Resilience

Elena's journey through infertility was marked by heartbreak and disappointment as she endured countless failed treatments and miscarriages. However, instead of allowing herself to be consumed by despair, Elena channeled her energy into cultivating resilience. She sought solace in the support of her partner and friends, finding strength in their unwavering love and encouragement. Through mindfulness practices and self-care rituals, Elena nurtured her spirit and found moments of peace amidst the storm. Though the road was fraught with obstacles, Elena's resilience ultimately led her to the precious gift of motherhood, proving that even in the face of adversity, hope prevails. Resilience is not a passive state but rather an active process of adaptation and growth in the face of adversity. It's the ability to bounce back from setbacks with newfound strength and determination, refusing to be defined by our circumstances. Cultivating resilience requires intentional practice and self-care, nurturing the body, mind, and spirit. Building a strong support network, engaging in activities that bring joy and fulfillment, and prioritizing self-compassion are essential components of resilience-building. By tending to our inner being through nurturing our physical, emotional, and spiritual well-being, we fortify ourselves against the storms of life and emerge stronger and more resilient than before.

Empowering Others Through Our Stories

As we navigate the terrain of pain and transformation, we have the power to inspire and uplift others through our stories. By sharing our experiences of resilience and triumph, we offer hope to those who may be traversing similar paths. Through acts of compassion and solidarity, we create a ripple effect of healing and empowerment that extends far beyond our individual experiences. Our willingness to show up authentically and vulnerably becomes a beacon of light in the darkness, guiding others toward their path of healing and empowerment.

Maya's journey through breast cancer was a testament to the power of vulnerability and resilience. Throughout her treatment, Maya documented her experiences in a blog, sharing candidly about the physical and emotional challenges she faced. Her words resonated with countless readers who found solace and inspiration in her journey. Maya's openness and authenticity not only empowered others to confront their struggles but also fostered a sense of community and connection among those navigating similar paths. In sharing her story, Maya discovered that her pain had the power to inspire healing and hope in others, transforming her journey from one of suffering to one of purpose and empowerment.

Embracing Your Journey - Rising Like a Phoenix

The journey will not be easy. There will be setbacks and moments of self-doubt. But remember, you are stronger than you think. Embrace your scars – they are a testament to your resilience, a reminder of all you've overcome. The experience has shaped you into the incredible woman you are today, compassionate, wise, and with a fire in your soul. You are not defined by your pain, but rather by how you choose to rise above it.

Conclusion

In this article, we have focused on how to discover and tap into the transformative power of pain. In our darkest moments, we have to unearth reservoirs of strength, courage, and resilience we never knew existed. By embracing vulnerability, finding meaning in adversity, and cultivating resilience, we can turn our pain into a source of power and inspiration. Let us embark on this journey together, knowing that within the depths of our suffering lies the potential for profound growth and healing. As we navigate the complexities of life, may we never forget the inherent strength and resilience that resides within each of us, waiting to be awakened and unleashed.

13

CONCLUSION

Conclusion: Feeling Like a Queen on Your Journey of Self-Love

As we conclude this exploration of self-love and the embrace of personal strength, remember: you are not just participating in life; you are reigning over your own rich, vibrant kingdom. Like a queen, every decision you make, every step you take, should reflect your majestic capacity for love, both for yourself and for others.

Start with the essentials - recognize that you might have vulnerabilities, areas where you feel less confident. Address them not with harsh judgment but with the compassion you would show a dear friend. Then, shift your focus to the abundance of your qualities, the areas where you excel and feel most proud. Let these drive your actions and fuel your self-belief.

As you move forward, carry yourself with the dignity of someone who knows her worth. Envision wearing a crown - each jewel represents a quality you love about yourself. Let this crown be a constant reminder of your royalty. In your kingdom, you set the rules. You decide who gets your time, your energy, and your heart. Choose wisely, and make sure they honor and uplift you as you deserve.

And remember, the journey of self-love is not selfish; it is essential. It is the wellspring from which all forms of love flow. By loving yourself, you teach other show to love you and set a standard for what you accept in your life. Embrace your role as a queen in your realm, walking with grace, ruling with compassion, and loving with all the strength of your royal heart.

Step forth from this book not just inspired but transformed. Feel empowered to love yourself, pursue your dreams, and create a life filled with joy, respect, and fulfillment. You are amazing, you are worthy, and above all, you are loved. Remember this always, and let it guide you through each day with confidence and pride.

In the grand finale of our journey together through the pages of this book, let this chapter serve as a manifesto for your life - a declaration of strength, self-love, and undying perseverance. Here, now, embrace the full measure of your potential and promise yourself never to step back into the shadows.

Be Strong, Stand Up for Yourself

To be strong does not only mean to endure; it means to stand firm, rooted in the belief of your own worth. Stand up for yourself. Let your voice echo with the truths you hold dear, and never allow the noise of the world to drown out your inner voice. Speaking your truth is not just a form of self-expression; it's a defense against those who would seek to diminish you. Your voice, your thoughts, your feelings - they matter.

Love Yourself, Set Goals, and Achieve Them

Self-love is the starting point of all great journeys. It fuels your drive to set ambitious goals and propels you towards achieving them. Love yourself with such depth and conviction that it becomes impossible not to strive for everything you deserve. Set your sights high, and then push higher. Every goal achieved is a testament to what you are capable of when your spirit is fueled by self-love.

Embrace Risk and Welcome Challenge

Never be afraid to take risks. The path less traveled is often the route to the most rewarding destinations. Risks challenge us to grow, to stretch beyond our current confines, and to truly see what we are capable of achieving. Embracing risk means embracing the possibility of failure - but also the limitless potential of success.

Protect Your Worth

Let this be clear: never, under any circumstances, allow anyone to abuse, belittle, put down, or disrespect you. You are a fortress of dignity and respect; let no one breach your walls. Always believe in yourself - even in moments when belief seems like a rare commodity. Your self-belief is your shield against the arrows of doubt and negativity.

Daily Affirmations

Anchor your days with affirmations that remind you of your strength and beauty:

- "I love me."
- "I'm unstoppable."
- "I'm beautiful."
- "I shall win. Period."

Repeat these words to yourself, for they are your battle cries in the quieter moments of self-doubt. They are your reminders that your love for yourself must be unwavering, especially in times when you feel alone. As you embark on this journey of self-discovery and empowerment, remember to nourish your mind, body, and spirit with boundless love and care. Speak daily affirmations to yourself, breathing life into your dreams and desires with each word uttered. "I love me, I'm unstoppable, I'm beautiful, and I shall win." Let these affirmations become the anthem of your soul, infusing every fiber of your being with unwavering confidence and empowerment.

And always remember, my dear queens: You are more than enough, just as you are. You are worthy of all the love, success, and happiness that the universe has to offer. So crown yourself with confidence, embrace your inner queen, and step boldly into the fullness of who you are. Your journey towards self-love and empowerment begins now - embrace it with open arms and a heart full of love. You are unstoppable. You are beautiful. And you shall win. Period!

Believe, Love, Dream, Achieve

Always believe in yourself. Always love yourself. Always follow your dreams. This trio of imperatives should be the guiding stars in the constellation of your life. Dream big, chase those dreams with fervor, and be open to experiencing new things. Each new experience is a stepping stone to greater wisdom and a fuller life.

Conclusion: A Powerful Send-Off

As we draw the curtains on this transformative narrative, remember that the end of this book marks not an ending but a commencement - the dawn of your personal odyssey. The chapters that lie ahead are blank pages waiting to be filled with your courage, wisdom, and the vibrancy of your spirit. You are fully equipped, brimming with potential and fortified by the profound discoveries you've made about yourself.

Empowered by Potential

Within you lies an immense potential, a reservoir of strength and capability that perhaps you've only begun to tap into. Every lesson imparted; every story told within these pages has been a tool to help you unlock that potential. Now, as you step beyond the written word into your reality, carry these tools with the confidence of someone who knows their true power.

You are more than ready. Ready to confront challenges with a resolute heart, to embrace opportunities with open arms, and to weave your aspirations into the fabric of your daily life. The narrative of your life is an epic waiting to be told in full, painted with bold strokes of perseverance, joy, and unyielding strength.

Living with Grace and Strength

Embrace each day with the grace of one who understands their worth. Grace is not just in the way you move but in how you respond to the world around you - with kindness, empathy, and a calm that comes from knowing you are at peace with yourself. Coupled with this grace is the unbreakable strength of character, forged through trials and triumphs alike. This strength is not characterized by rigidity or inflexibility but by a profound resilience, a will to go on, that springs eternal from within your heart.

You are unbreakable, not because you never face hardship, but because you have learned to rise every time you fall. You understand that each setback is not a finale but a setup for a greater comeback.

The Spirit of the Unstoppable

What truly sets you apart is the spirit of one who is unstoppable. Your journey through self-love and empowerment has ignited a fire within - a fire that fuels your passion for life and drives you to pursue your greatest dreams. Embrace this unstoppable spirit. Let it propel you through barriers and past limits imposed by others or by circumstances.

As you move forward, remember that your life is an extraordinary tale of overcoming and becoming. Each day offers a new scene in your epic story. Approach each scene with enthusiasm and a proactive stance, ready to be the protagonist who shapes their fate with deliberate, thoughtful actions.

The Crown of Self-Respect and Love

Walk with your head held high, crowned with the self-respect and love you have cultivated through your journey. This crown is not visible to the eye but felt by the heart. It influences how you see yourself and dictates how you interact with the world. It is a crown that enhances your dignity, commands respect, and radiates your inner beauty.

The love you've nurtured for yourself is your shield and strength. It filters out negativity and bathes you in light, attracting those who respect and admire yourself - worth. It compels you to act in ways that consistently affirm your values and your essence.

Radiating Your Light

The world awaits the luminescence of your presence. Each step you take is a beacon for others, a testament to the power of transformation through self-love and resilience. Do not dim your light; let it shine brightly. Radiate positivity, hope, and the possibility of renewal. Through your actions, inspire others to embark on their journeys of self-discovery and empowerment.

In your hands lies the pen that will script your future. With every word you write, with every action you take, you are crafting a legacy of strength, grace, and unstoppable spirit. Go forth into the world with your head held high, your heart open, and your spirit untamed.

Embrace your life as it unfolds, with all its unpredictability and splendor. Live passionately, love deeply, and leave a trail of light that others can follow. You are ready now. Go on, radiate your unique brilliance into the world. Embrace your story, live your truth, and enjoy every moment of this magnificent journey.

As we close this book, remember that its pages are just the beginning of your story. The chapters ahead of you are yours to write. You are equipped, empowered, and enlivened by your own potential. Go forward with the grace of one who knows their worth, the strength of one who is unbreakable, and the spirit of one who is unstoppable.

You are ready now. Ready to live your best life, ready to embrace each day with passion and purpose, ready to be the protagonist of your own epic tale. Walk with your head held high, crowned with the self-respect and love you've cultivated. The world is waiting for you to shine your light. Go on, radiate!

About The Author

Unique Parsha, known affectionately as Pinky, is an inspirational author, mentor, and passionate advocate for self-love and personal growth, inspiring girls and women globally to embrace their individuality with confidence. Recognized as "**The Pink Lady of Oakland**," her vibrant persona mirrors her unyielding passion for all things pink and shares a powerful message of self-love through her interactive platform, **www.thepinkladyofoakland.com**.

With a diverse academic background encompassing Sociology, Human Services, Fashion Design, and Psychology from the prestigious San Francisco State University and other colleges, Unique's commitment to knowledge and societal impact knows no bounds. Certified as a Domestic Violence Counselor, Therapist, and Anger Management Counselor, she lends her expertise to the National Crisis Line of America and supports victims of domestic violence.

An impactful figure in her community, Unique collaborates with local law enforcement to combat human trafficking and actively mentors youth in educational institutions and juvenile facilities. She also lends a hand with teen shelters working with pregnant teen girls, and domestic violence shelters working with domestic violence victims. Founder and

CEO of *Love N Me*, Unique established the nonprofit organization, dedicated to empowering girls and women to embrace self-love, discover their self-worth, and find purpose in life.

She also owns a credit repair company called Unique Credit Fix, a marketing company called Pink Lady Marketing, and a brand called The Pink Lady Of Oakland.

Driven by a genuine desire to impact a wider audience, Unique has authored a transformative book, I Must Love Me. Through personal experiences, valuable insights, and profound wisdom, she inspires women of all ages to embrace their uniqueness, love themselves unconditionally, and unlock their true potential for limitless possibilities.

Beyond her professional endeavors, Unique's interests and pastimes align with her mission to spread love and positivity. Her passion for music, singing, and dancing is palpable while her affinity for shopping for pink things warms her heart. Also her pink-themed house to.

Made in the USA
Columbia, SC
27 May 2024

69bcb829-c945-4c9e-a21a-8ff4fcf94480R01